MY MASTER'S SEVENFOLD PLAN

David Hamshire

MY MASTER'S SEVENFOLD PLAN

*The words the LORD are pure words,
Like silver tried in a furnace of earth,
Purified seven times.*

*You shall keep them, O LORD,
You shall preserve them
from this generation forever.*

(Psalm 12:6–7).

Copyright 2025 David Hamshire

The right of David Hamshire to be identified as the author of this work has been asserted by him in accordance with the Copyright, Designs and Patents Act 1988.

All rights reserved. No part of this book may be reproduced or transmitted in any form or by any means, electronic or mechanical, including photocopying, recording, or by any information storage and retrieval system, without prior permission in writing from the author.

Unless otherwise stated, all Scripture quotations are taken from the NEW KING JAMES VERSION ®. Copyright © 1982 by Thomas Nelson, Inc. Used by permission. All rights reserved.

Where stated, the Scripture taken from the JEWISH STUDY BIBLE (J.S.B.) TANAKH TRANSLATION. Used by permission. All rights reserved worldwide.

Cover design by Andrew Starritt, TLB Direct, 3-6 Blackworth Court, Highworth, Swindon, /Wiltshire, SN6 7NS, U.K.

Printed and Published in the U.K. by:
Origin Zone
14 Ergo Business Park
Kelvin Road
Swindon
SN3 3JW

To contact the author, please email:
david.hamshire@uwclub.net

CONTENTS

ACKNOWLEDGEMENTS 7

AUTHOR'S NOTES 9

FOREWORD 11

THE POWER OF THE HIGHEST 13

PREFACE 15

PART ONE

PAR EXCELLENCE 19

FROM DUST, TO DUST 29

THE MASTER CRAFTSMAN 35

PART TWO

THE FIRST DAY, THE FIRST APPOINTED TIME OF THE
LORD, THE FIRST PILLAR OF WISDOM 45

THE SECOND DAY, THE SECOND APPOINTED TIME OF THE
LORD, THE SECOND PILLAR OF WISDOM 63

THE THIRD DAY, THE THIRD APPOINTED TIME OF THE
LORD, THE THIRD PILLAR OF WISDOM 75

THE FOURTH DAY, THE FOURTH APPOINTED TIME OF THE
LORD, THE FOURTH PILLAR OF WISDOM 85

THE FIFTH DAY, THE FIFTH APPOINTED TIME OF THE
LORD, THE FIFTH PILLAR OF WISDOM 99

CONTENTS

THE SIXTH DAY, THE SIXTH APPOINTED TIME OF THE
LORD, THE SIXTH PILLAR OF WISDOM 109

THE SEVENTH DAY, THE SEVENTH APPOINTED TIME OF THE
LORD, THE SEVENTH PILLAR OF WISDOM 133

MY MASTER'S SEVENFOLD PLAN 143

THE MARRIAGE SUPPER OF THE SON OF GOD 145

A. WISEMAN 147

THE SARAJEVO HAGGADAH 149

THOU DIDST LEAVE THY THRONE 157

BIBLIOGRAPHY 159

****

ACKNOWLEDGMENTS

First I thank Jesus, the One who the Bible acknowledges as being the *'Master Craftsman'*. Although I will never know the full extent of His help, I am aware that without it what is contained within these pages would have been impossible.

I also thank Janet, a friend when we were at school together in the mid to late 1950s, then from when we were married in 1966 my chosen lifelong companion, for accompanying me on our journey through life. Before we were married, Janet gave me a copy of CRUDEN'S CONCORDANCE and inside the front cover she wrote: *"Read, mark, learn and inwardly digest His Word."* Janet, I would have been lost without it.

In 1967 (on our first anniversary), Janet gave me a copy of MATTHEW HENRY'S COMMENTARY OF THE WHOLE BIBLE. This time she wrote inside the front cover: *"The Lord hath done great thing for us whereof we are glad."* (Psalm 126:3). Henry's Commentary has also been a close companion.

I thank Desi Maxwell whose ministry I have benefited from, for writing the Foreword. Desi has studied at the University of Ulster and the Westminster and Princeton Theological Seminaries. He entered pastoral ministry for seven years – three in Canada and four in Belfast. For twenty years, Desi lectured at the Belfast Bible College before seeking to bring the classroom to the living room through *'Xplorations'*, the ministry he co-founded and directs with his wife Heather.

Given his academic and teaching background, Desi's kind words are more than I could have hoped for and I am very grateful for his positive comments.

My thanks also include Dr. Ron George, from Crowborough, East Sussex, who with his wife Nancy are the founders of the Eurasia Education Foundation.

In 2016 (again in 2017), Dr. George invited me to accompany him to Chișinău, the capital of Moldova, to lecture to students at a Christian University on the subject of *'The Hebrew Roots Of The Christian Faith'*. This study has evolved partly as a result of Dr. George's kind invitations.

I also thank Bob Mawer, a friend who lives in Shrivenham, Oxfordshire, for proof-reading the manuscript for this book. When I asked Bob for his help, he was very willing and I thank him for pointing out a number of errors and making other helpful suggestions for the improvement of this study. Any remaining errors are my responsibility and I'm very sorry if you encounter them.

****

AUTHOR'S NOTES

The reason I quote the NEW KING JAMES VERSION (NKJV) of the Bible for all but two of the Scriptures I refer to, is because it is my preferred translation. Unlike some translations, the NKJV is based on ancient manuscripts that are known as *'Textus Receptus'* (Received Text). In the NJKV, God's name in the Old Testament is represented by the consonants YHWH – (*Yodh-He-Wa-He*). In Hebrew, *'The Tetragrammaton'*, they are translated as LORD, or GOD (using capital letters). This pattern has been followed throughout the history of the KING JAMES BIBLE. This form of capitals is also used in the New Testament for passages quoted from the Old Testament.

Where I quote from Scripture, I have done so by using italics. In some places I have set words or phrases in bold to add emphasis. One example of this is Proverbs 8:30. Here the contributor refers to Himself as a *'Master Craftsman'* (or, *'One brought up.'*). This is just one of many occasions when we are introduced (prophetically) to Jesus – of whom it was also said by the Psalmist quoting God as being His Father: *"You are My Son, today I became Your Father."* (Psalm 2:7).

It would not surprise me if some of my thoughts were to be challenged – such as the *'Today'* God refers to in Psalm two. Why, then, have I sought to publish this study?

At age fifteen (1959), I enlisted in the Royal Air Force and from 1964–1970 helped to maintain its fleet of four-engined Bristol Britannia aircraft. On one occasion I was tasked with taking part in an air test and after departure from Lyneham in Wiltshire, the Captain reported faults with three of the four engines! Though we were not in any immediate danger, because of the sub-zero conditions and the serious risk of wing-icing, our return to Lyneham was no longer possible.

Faced with a diversion to north Wales, I asked the Captain if he would allow me to investigate – to which he agreed. The first thing to do was to consult the aircraft's wiring diagrams. This led me to suspect that three engine-operated devices which controlled the aircraft's anti-icing systems had failed; however with the Captain's permission I believed I could electrically over-ride the three devices. The Captain asked me if it was safe to do so. I replied: *"Yes Sir, trust me!"*

At 10,000 feet and aided by the aircraft's wiring diagrams, I set to work in the freight bay below the cabin floor to re-wire from inside the aircraft, the three devices. On replacing the fuses for the three circuits, the anti-icing systems worked perfectly and we were able to return safely to Lyneham. My success was due solely to the fact I had with me my tools, a torch, and a complete set of the aircraft's wiring diagrams.

Over many years I have learnt the same is true of the Bible. The apostle Paul was aware of this principle and of how it applied to God's written word the Bible. Paul wrote:

> ***All*** *Scripture is given by inspiration of God, and is profitable for doctrine, for reproof, for correction, for instruction in righteousness, that the man of God may be complete, thoroughly equipped for every good work.* (2 Timothy 3:16–17).

Having learnt how to fix electrical problems, I pray this study will help you as you read the Bible. In early 1964, just seven words from this book saved me from myself. (See John 3:30).

David Hamshire
2025

FOREWORD

Bible-readers and jam-makers often adopt similar methods. Despite the apparent difference in the two occupations, the inclination is to store the fruits of their labours in neatly sealed units. Readers tend to systematize their findings and file them away in neatly organized mental compartments, while cooks use jam jars to ensure the flavours never mix!

Maybe this is a wise decision when it comes to jam making, but it is dreadfully debilitating when it comes to exploring the richness of the Bible.

While we stand indebted to many scholars, much academic study of the Bible is specialized. An *'Expert'* on the Hebrew Bible is not allowed to comment on the New Testament, and vice versa. Such is the degree of specialization the view of the sweeping forest has been obscured by the twigs on the trees.

The outcome is to the detriment of us all.

The fact that Hebrew, the language of the Scriptures, has no word for theology, doctrine or creed, surely alerts us to something? All our attempts to *'organize'* the Bible into rigidly systematic units are rather meaningless. Surely, it's time to take a step back and to look at the text as a whole?

Abraham Heschel once observed that the Greek studies to understand, while the Hebrew studies to revere. Our reverence, and indeed our awe, will certainly only increase as we grow in sensitivity to interconnections of time, place and people in this unique literature.

This is what David does in these pages. It's as if he invites us to don a new pair of tri-focals to see with excitement that no one text can be studied in isolation. No one angle, neither time, place, nor people, will provide us with a definitive interpretation, but all three combine to give us a high definition insight.

The rabbis were often masterful at this and their method sets them apart from our traditional western methods.

As you journey with David, you won't find everything sitting neatly labelled on shelves, ordered with the precision we've come to expect. That is simply not the way the Bible was intended to be read.

I invite you to travel with David as he discards the old containers and lets the richness of the flavours mix.

Desi Maxwell

THE POWER OF THE HIGHEST

At a pivotal moment in time – chosen by none other than God Himself – the angel Gabriel visited a city in Galilee named Nazareth. It was here that God's Chief Messenger spoke to a young woman whose name was Mary.

The following is what Gabriel said Mary.

"The Holy Spirit will come upon you,
And the power of the Highest will overshadow you;
Therefore, also, that Holy One who is to be born,
Will be called the Son of God."

(Luke 1:35)

About forty weeks later – the timing was crucial:

And she [Mary] brought forth her firstborn Son,
And wrapped Him in swaddling cloths,
And laid Him in a manger,
Because there was no room for them in the inn.

(Luke 2:7).

****

PREFACE

From Proverbs 8:30, we learn that Jesus is in full conformity with His Father in their homologous relationship.

"Then I was beside Him as a master craftsman."

During His time of ministry, *'...the common people heard Him gladly'* and they often referred to Jesus as Master. Master can mean teacher and/or authority for one's calling. Therefore, when reviewing my Master's Sevenfold Plan, it is essential we see Jesus as being an essential Figure in His Father's Plan.

Although it is tempting to dwell on the New Testament about Jesus' calling, prophets featured in the Old Testament wrote a great deal more. For example, one of the most descriptive prophecies about Jesus is the opening phrase in Psalm 22. Written a thousand years before it took place, this prophecy quotes the anguish Jesus was to utter from the cross:

"My God, My God, why have you forsaken Me?"

An important aspect of the Old Testament prophets is that so many of them wrote about Jesus. This is why when Jesus was making His way up to Jerusalem, He recalled *'All'* that the prophets had written about Him. Jesus said:

"And all things that are written by the prophets concerning the Son of Man will be accomplished." (Luke 18:31).

Prophets were those who by the leading and guidance of the Holy Spirit, recorded messages not only on God's behalf for their own generation, but also for every future generation.

In his book REVEALING JESUS AS MESSIAH, Dr. Stuart Sacks writes about what Isaiah wrote concerning Jesus in what is known as the FOUR SERVANT SONGS. (Isaiah 42:1-9; 49:1-7; 50:4-11; and 52:13-53:12). Dr. Sacks – who is Jewish and well-placed to comment on this vital subject – explains:

> Much of the Servant's work is couched in what is called the PROPHETIC PERFECT, a way of Hebraic writing which describes a future event as if it has already happened.

Examples of the PROPHETIC PERFECT can be seen in how many of the Biblical prophets wrote about Jesus. Two well-known examples are included in what Isaiah wrote.

1. *"The LORD **has** called Me from the womb; from the matrix of My mother He **has** made mention of My name."* (Isaiah 49:1).

2. *For He **was** cut off from the land of the living; for the transgressions of My people He **was** stricken.* (Isaiah 53:8).

Here Isaiah describes Jesus' birth and His death as if they had already occurred, yet in a PROPHETIC PERFECT idiom these events were not to take place until many years had passed. Friedrich Gesenius – (1786-1842) – has said how PERFECTUM PROPHETICUM (Latin for PROPHETIC PERFECT), though not widely understood by most Gentiles, is a vital element when it comes to understanding the Old Testament.

In FIGURES OF SPEECH USED IN THE BIBLE, E. W. Bullinger explains how the switch from the future tense to the past tense is the figure of speech HETEROSIS. The past is used instead of the future to emphasize the certainty of an event. The PROPHETIC PERFECT is how prophecies about Jesus in the Old Testament should be read and understood.

A further example (but in an allegorical form with additional examples occurring throughout Scripture) is in what Joshua said when his life was drawing to a close. Joshua was the man who God had chosen to take over from Moses, the leadership of the children of Israel before they crossed the River Jordan to enter the Promised Land.

Knowing he would not be around for much longer, Joshua was concerned that once he had died the people would turn to other gods; such as the gods which the surrounding nations worshipped. Joshua had already said to his people:

"And if it seems evil to you to serve the LORD, choose for yourselves this day whom you will serve, whether the gods which your fathers served that were on the other side of the River, or the gods of the Amorites, in whose land you dwell. But as for me and my house, we will serve the LORD." (Joshua 24:15).

Having taken in what Joshua had said to them, about the danger of turning to other gods, the people replied to Joshua:

"Far be it from us that we should forsake the LORD to serve other gods..." "The LORD our God we will serve, and His voice we will obey!" (Joshua 24:16 & 24).

Mindful of the capricious nature of some among the children of Israel, Joshua, it seems, wanted to ensure that his warning would not go unheeded. To allay his concerns, *'Then Joshua wrote these words in the Book of the Law of God.'*

And he took a large stone, and set it up there under the oak that was by the sanctuary of the LORD. [This sanctuary could easily have been Israel's Ark of the Covenant which was symbolic of God's dwelling place]. *And Joshua said to all the people, "Behold, this stone shall be a witness to us,* *for it has **heard** all the words of the LORD which He spoke to us. It* [that is: *'This Stone'*] *shall therefore be a witness to you, lest you **deny** your God."* (Joshua 24:26–27).

In what appears to have been a whimsical decision, a *'Large Stone'* that Joshua seems to have selected at random; it had *'Heard'* all that God had said. Was Joshua declaring in a PROPHETIC PERFECT idiom, that this *'Large Stone'* which he then placed next to the *'Sanctuary of the LORD'*, had a veiled and dignified function in contributing to God's presence?

Jesus, who on one occasion quoted from Psalm 118:22–23 which refers to a stone, implied that this *'Prophetic Stone'* was none other than a representation of Himself. Jesus said:

"The stone which the builders rejected has become the chief cornerstone. [Being a cornerstone suggests it was a large and wholesome stone]. *This was the LORD's doing; and it is marvellous in our eyes."* (Matthew 21:42).

This *'Chief Cornerstone'* is the Lord Jesus. (1 Peter 2:6–8). For those who saw themselves as the custodians of religion, yet they denied Jesus the right to live, their denial was as Joshua had warned: *"...lest you **deny** your God"*. Regarding the form of this prophetic stone, Isaiah once prophesied to all Israel.

*"The LORD of hosts, Him you shall hallow; let Him be your fear, and let Him be your dread. He will be as a sanctuary, but a **stone of stumbling and a rock of offence** to both the houses of Israel..."* (Isaiah 8:13–14).

Not only is Jesus a *'Sanctuary'*, a dwelling place – as He is also linked with Israel's Tabernacle, the Holy-of Holies and its Ark of the Covenant – He is also a *'Stone of Stumbling and a Rock of Offence'* to those who **deny** He is the Son of God. See also Psalm 22:6– 8 and Mathew 27:41–43.

PART ONE

PAR EXCELLENCE

For my Master's Plan to achieve its objective, first we must consider the Lunar Calendar as observed by Jewish people, versus the Solar Calendar as observed by Gentiles. Months in the Lunar Calendar are fixed to the time it takes for the Moon (our travelling companion) to orbit the Earth. These months are known as Synodic Months. For the Solar Calendar, it follows the time taken for the Earth and the Moon to orbit the Sun. A complete orbit of the Sun equates to a Solar Year.

The Lunar Calendar therefore is tied to the movement of the Moon as it orbits the Earth, when each lunation lasts for twenty-nine days, twelve hours, forty-four minutes and three seconds. What is the ultimate in precision is that the Moon, which is fixed vertically on its north and south poles, **turns on its axis by exactly the same amount of time as it takes for the Moon to orbit the Earth.** This is why we *never* see the back of the Moon, only what is known as the Moon's Face. Visually, the *'Moon's Appearance'*, to borrow a phrase from Hebrews 13:8, **'Is the same yesterday, today, and forever'**.

For those who have sent cameras to photograph the back of the Moon, they have discovered that as with the Moon's Face – which we can see clearly from the Earth and the battering it has received from a plethora of objects – that the back of the Moon has also been battered in a similar way. A basic enquiry could easily be: *"Why has the Moon been battered in this way but not the Earth?"*

A Lunar Year – usually it consists of twelve Lunar months – alternates between months of twenty-nine days (months with even numbers), and months of thirty days (months with uneven numbers). This means that the Moon's cycle of twelve Lunar months lasts for three hundred and fifty-four days – which is approximately eleven days shorter than a Solar Year.

In order to correct this anomaly, so the Lunar Calendar does not get out of phase with the Earth's agricultural seasons, every two/three years an extra month is added to the Lunar Calendar to bring it into line with the Solar Calendar. This adjustment is made seven times in every nineteen year cycle.

An important reason for making these seven adjustments is to ensure that not only the Lunar Year keeps in phase with the astronomical seasons, but also the Jewish people's main religious festivals – their Seven Annual Appointed Times of the LORD – take place at the correct times in the year.

A Solar Year consists of three hundred and sixty-five days, five hours, forty-eight minutes and forty-five seconds for the Earth and the Moon to orbit the Sun. The distance travelled is approximately five hundred and eighty four million miles. For some this may seem unbelievable – yet it is true.

If two children were playing in the Republic of the Congo – a central African country which spans the equator – without their awareness they would be travelling at one thousand miles-per-hour in the direction of the Earth's rotation of its axis. They would also be travelling at sixty-seven-thousand-miles-per-hour in their journey around the Sun! Yet for the majority of people, Divine acceptance is noted by its absence.

It is within this set-piece order of Creation that these cycles of time take place, and over prolonged periods. If they failed to maintain their positions in the way they have been set, we would not be here. Life in the sequence as it was Created since time immemorial would be impossible.

Brian E. Cox, CBE, FRS, Professor of Particle Physics at the School of Physics and Astronomy at the University of Manchester, has said to his many devotes who follow Professor Cox in his scientific lectures on television:

"The Solar System is driven by rhythms so regular that the whole thing could be run by clockwork. It seems extraordinary that such a well ordered system could have come into being spontaneously, but it is in fact a great example of the beauty and symmetry that lies at the heart of the universe."

Professor Cox is correct: The Solar System is extraordinary. But if it had been left to evolution, it is inconceivable it could have happened in the way that it did, or that it remains so. Therefore the Sun, Moon and the Earth must be God's work, for as Professor Cox has clearly intimated: **"His beauty and His symmetry lies at the heart of the universe."** Is this why when God saw everything that He had made, that He said: *"...and indeed it was very good."* (Genesis 1:31)?

God's Plan as outlined in Genesis 1:1–2:3 which describes a period of Seven Days, is that we might understand who His Master Craftsman is: His Son the Lord Jesus. And just before the Word of God became a man in human flesh, an angel of the Lord appeared to Joseph in a dream – himself a master craftsman – to inform him: *"...you shall call His name JESUS, for He will save His people from their sins."* (Matthew 1:21).

Shortly before Jesus died – *'Now it came to pass, when the time had come for Him to be received up, that He steadfastly set His **face** to go to Jerusalem, and sent messengers before His* *face*' (Luke 9:51-52) - He was acutely aware of what was about to take place. He would be flogged by Roman soldiers and His *face* would become as battered and bruised as the Moon's face in appearance after being so terribly beaten.

Today, a simile of the bruising suffered by Jesus can be seen in the Moon's lunar seas of dark basaltic lavas which are identifiable from every dwelling place on Earth. When Isaiah was writing of the days to come and the abuse Jesus would one day suffer, he was inspired to write:

"Just as many were astonished at you, so His visage [His face] *was marred more than any man, and His form more than the sons of men; so shall He sprinkle* [startle] *many nations. Kings shall shut their mouths at Him; for what had not been told them they shall see, and what they had not heard they shall consider."* (Isaiah 52:14-15).

In the next chapter of this his fourth Servant Song, Isaiah informs his readers - hundreds of years before it took place - about why Jesus' face was to become so terribly bruised.

"But He was wounded for our transgressions, He was bruised for our iniquities; the chastisement for our peace was upon Him, and by His stripes we are healed." (Isaiah 53:5).

Continuing and adding to in the next sentence, Isaiah adds to his prophecy by describing our common predicament.

'All we like sheep have gone astray; we have turned, every one, to his own way; and the LORD *has laid on Him the iniquity of us all.'* (Isaiah 53:6).

The suffering Jesus endured was because of our tendency to veer away from God, but in wanting us to draw near to Him,

His Son was *'...led as a lamb to the slaughter.'* This is why *'...it pleased the LORD to bruise Him.'* (Isaiah 53:7 & 10).

God's response, *'...it pleased the LORD to bruise Him,'* – is this not an unexpected response? How can it be pleasurable for any father to see his son so berated and vilified? Perhaps the reason is disclosed in the New Testament book of Hebrews?

"Therefore we also, since we are surrounded by so great a cloud of witnesses [See Hebrews chapter 11], *let us lay aside every weight, and the sin which so easily ensnares us, and let us run with endurance the race that is set before us, looking unto Jesus, the author and finisher of our faith, who for the joy* [the pleasure] *that was set before Him endured the cross, despising the shame, and has sat down at the right hand of the throne of God."* (Hebrews 12:1-2).

The *'Joy'* Jesus foresaw was that having endured the cross, then for those who would become His advocates, they would experience the radiance and the splendour of God's love.

For the Sun – which is four hundred times the diameter of the Moon and four hundred times the distance the Moon is from the Earth – when fully eclipsed (when the Moon passes between the Sun and the Earth), its appearance on Earth is of the Sun being equal in size to the Moon. This is no accident.

It is during a complete Solar Eclipse – when the protection afforded by the Moon is present when its shadow is passing over the Earth – that it is relatively safe to look to the Sun and study the Sun's Corona; its crown of light that extends far out into space. Corona is the Latin word for Crown.

In Psalm 91:1, we read of those who dwell in the secret place of the Most High, that they *'...shall abide under the shadow* [or the protection] *of the Almighty.'*

In 2019 when a Corona virus pandemic became so deadly with its spiked shaped virus that replicated a crown – referred to by the U.K. Prime Minister Boris Johnson as: *"This devilish illness"* – its name became something of an enigma.

Primarily to aid us in our being adopted by God and in our response to love and to honour Him, God's servant Isaiah wrote of two Crowns/Coronas:

> *Woe to the crown* [Corona] *of pride,* [it] *is a fading flower.*

But for those who seek after God and are penitent:

> *The* LORD *of hosts will be for a crown* [Corona] *of glory and a diadem of beauty to the remnant of His people.* (See Isaiah chapter 28, verses 1–5).

Jesus also made reference to a similar enigma – that in 2020 as face coverings that were once the trade-mark of a thief became an international requirement as the Corona virus threatened the lives of millions of people – when He said:

> *"I am the door. If anyone enters by Me, he will be saved, and will go in and out and find pasture. The thief* [as with the Corona virus] *does not come except to steal, and to kill, and to destroy. I have come that they may have life, and that they may have it more abundantly."* (John 10:9–10).

It is because God is resplendent in majesty and holiness that we are unable to look upon God's face. However, in Malachi 4:2, Jesus is described as *'The Sun of Righteousness'*. Also in Revelation 1:16, Jesus' countenance, His face, is described as *'The Sun shining in its strength'*. This is one of the reasons why God sent His Son; for Him to reflect the majesty of His Father and who when speaking in the Temple of the last days when the harvest of His people will be gathered in, said:

"And there will be signs in the sun, in the moon, and in the stars; and on the earth distress of nations, with perplexity, the sea and the waves roaring; men's hearts failing them from fear and the expectation of those things which are coming on the earth, for the powers of the heavens will be shaken. Then they will see the Son of Man coming in a cloud with power and great glory. Now when these things begin to happen, look up [to the Son] and lift up your heads, because your redemption draws near." (Luke 21:25–28).

Meanwhile, David, having studied the waxing and the waning of the Moon when caring for his father's sheep, concluded:

The heavens declare the glory of God; and the firmament shows His handiwork. Day unto day utters speech, and night unto night reveals knowledge. ... In them He has set a tabernacle [or Tent] *for the sun, which is like a bridegroom coming out of his chamber.* (Psalm 19:1–2 & 4b–5).

The apostle Paul also knew of the Solar and Lunar chemistry of the Fourth Day when he wrote to those in the Church in Corinth of their glory. Paul describes their glory as:

There is one glory of the sun, another glory of the moon, and another glory of the stars; for one star differs from another star in glory. (1 Corinthians 15:41). See Genesis 1:14–19.

What might be a little pedantic for language purists, are the repeats the Psalmist employs to describe the par-excellence of the Sun, the Moon, and the stars, and how in themselves they bring praise to God. In Psalm 148:1–5 we read:

Praise the LORD! Praise the LORD from the heavens; Praise Him in the heights! Praise Him, all His angels; Praise Him all His hosts! Praise Him, sun and moon; Praise Him, all you stars of light! Praise Him, you heavens of heavens, and you waters above the heavens! Let them praise the name of the LORD, for He commanded and they were created.

In fact there are a number of announcements in the Bible that proclaim God with the Sun and Jesus with the Moon: the Moon that reflects the light of the Sun as Jesus in a similar mode reflects the light, glory, and majesty of His Father.

For example, in Psalm seventy two we read:

> He will bring justice to the poor of the people; He will save the children of the needy, and will break in pieces the oppressor. They shall fear You as long as the sun and moon endure throughout all generations. (Psalm 72:4–5).

In his commentary on Psalm 72, Rev. Eric Lane points out:

> The references to the Sun, the Moon and all generations clearly go beyond any human king; even the Lord's anointed, and find their fulfilment in the reign of Christ.

And in Psalm eighty four, we read:

> "For the LORD God is a sun and shield; the LORD will give grace and glory; no good thing will He withhold from those who walk uprightly." (Psalm 84:11).

The way the Sun radiates its merit by its light and its heat, so God radiates Himself into the lives of those who honour Him. This applies unreservedly to the world's two people groups. 1, Those who are simple. 2, Those who lack understanding. (These two people groups will become much clearer later). And in James 1:17, God's merit is described as being:

> Every good gift ... comes down from the Father of lights with whom there is no variation or shadow of turning.

As a paradigm in the way that Jesus was destined to reflect the light and majesty of His Father, Zacharias, the father of John the Baptist (who was born approximately six months before Jesus), once said about his own son's ministry:

> *"And you, child, will be called the prophet of the Highest; for you will go before the **face** of the Lord to prepare His ways, to give knowledge of salvation to His people by the remission of their sins, through the tender mercy of our God, with which the Dayspring [i.e., The Dawn] from on high has visited us; to give light to those who sit in darkness and the shadow of death, to guide our feet into the way of peace."* (Luke 1:76-79). The *'Dayspring from on high'* is Jesus.

In the Bible there are many allegorical symbols. But – and this is consequential – this means we should never think of created things (including man-made *'Things'* made from the elements of Creation and which will always pass away) and elevate and honour them to a degree which was never intended, and which is both idolatrous and sinful.

Moses, once described as being a humble man to whom God spoke to face-to-face for he was faithful (Numbers 12:3-8), knew of this oblique danger, and so he warned God's people the children of Israel:

> *"And take heed, lest you lift your eyes to heaven, and when you see the sun, the moon, and the stars, all the host of heaven, you feel driven to worship them and serve them, which the LORD your God has given to all the peoples under the whole heaven as a heritage."* (Deuteronomy 4:19).

Rather than revering the Sun, the Moon and the stars as objects of our worship (as decreed by Pharaoh Akhenaten who forbade the worship of gods other than the Sun – the worship of one god but not denying that other gods do exist

– which was later seen as being heretical and henotheistic when Pharaoh Tutankhamen annulled Akhenaten's decree), though in Scripture they may be identified as emblematic, true worship is when we worship God in spirit and in truth, the Originator of these heavenly bodies. (John 4:24).

Regarding the worship of material made things – which can so easily lead to an erratic lifestyle – the parable Jesus used to highlight this danger was of a rich man who set his heart on acquiring many possessions, then to his deep and painful sorrow came to realise he had nowhere to store them!

As a result he took a rather naïve decision to pull down his existing properties in order to build larger ones in which to store his possessions (instead of donating them to charity!). Having done so, he relaxed. He then said to himself:

> *"Soul, you have many goods laid up for many years; take your ease; eat, drink and be merry."* (Luke 12:19).

Is this not a classic example of not only too many goods, but also too many gods? And so Jesus said of him:

> *"God said to him, 'Fool'! This night your soul will be required of you; then whose will those things be which you have provided?"* (Luke 12:20).

SEVEN DAYS

For generations it has been widely known that a seven day week is a faultless scale for our health and our physiological welfare. What is reassuring about God's Plan is that it is one that has never needed change. In the Hebrew perception of numbers, seven is seen as being: 'SPIRITUAL PERFECTION'.

****

FROM DUST TO DUST

Before we trace my Master's Sevenfold Plan, included in God's Plan is a description of how we came to be here. Unlike evolution, I agree with David the Psalmist.

"For You formed my inward parts; You covered me [in skin] *in my mother's womb. I will praise You, for I am fearfully and wonderfully made; marvellous are Your works, and that my soul knows very well."* (Psalm 139:13–14).

To believe otherwise – not forgetting gender heterogeneity that has enabled life to continue unabated from the time of Creation – is cause for tried and tested scrutiny. Though I do accept that limited changes in some mutations can occur, I cannot accept that animal primates mutated to become Homo-sapiens! Intelligent design is the way David perceived and understood Creation and I entirely agree with him.

PRIMAL DUST

It is not until Genesis 2:4 that we can begin to read about the second account of Creation. This account differs a great deal from the first account. See Genesis 1:1–2:3. It includes:

And the LORD *God formed man of the dust of the ground, and breathed into his nostrils the breath of life; and man became a living being.* (Genesis 2:7).

But before God formed man, in Proverbs 8:26 we read:

"While as yet He had not made the earth or the fields, or the primal dust of the world."

Primal dust, derived from the sources God identified for the making of a man in His image, is confirmed in Psalm 103:14.

For He [that is the LORD our God] *knows our frame;* **He remembers that we are dust.**

In Bill Bryson's book, THE BODY – A GUIDE FOR OCCUPANTS, Bryson addresses the make-up of just a single human cell.

You could call together all the brainiest people who are alive now, or have ever lived, and endow them with the complete sum of human knowledge, and they could not between them make a single living cell. That is unquestionably the most astounding thing about us – that we are just a collection of inert components, the same stuff you would find in a pile of dirt.

Almost certainly – and maybe without realising it – Bryson has affirmed the accuracy of the Bible: '...*the* LORD *God formed man of the dust of the ground.*' (Genesis 2:7).

To assist those whose faith in God is like a grain of mustard seed (Matthew 17:20), our Maker's selection has now been confirmed by the Royal Society of Chemistry. Scientists now know that 99.1% of the mass of the human body is made up of just six elements. In alphabetical order they are Calcium, Carbon, Hydrogen, Oxygen, Nitrogen and Phosphorus. In the ensuing descriptions, I thank the Royal Society of Chemistry for their help in my summarising of these six elements.

CALCIUM – Calcium is the fifth most common element in the Earth's crust, and the third most abundant metal. The most common calcium compound is calcium carbonate, found in limestone and the fossilised remnants of early sea life. Gypsum, anhydrite, fluorite and apatite are also sources of calcium.

CARBON – Carbon is the 15th most abundant element in the Earth's crust, and the fourth most common element in the universe by mass after hydrogen, helium, and oxygen. Carbon's abundance, its unique diversity of organic compounds, and its unusual ability to form polymers at the temperatures commonly encountered on Earth, enables this element to serve as a common element of all known life. It is the second most abundant element in the human body by mass (about 18.5%) after oxygen.

HYDROGEN – Hydrogen is the most abundant chemical substance in the universe, constituting roughly 75% of all normal matter. Stars, such as our Sun, are mainly composed of hydrogen in the plasma state. Most of the hydrogen on the Earth exists in molecular forms, such as water and organic compounds. For the most common isotope of hydrogen (symbol ^1H), each atom has one proton, one electron, but no neutrons.

NITROGEN – Nitrogen is a non-metal and the lightest member of group fifteen of the periodic table, often called the pnictogens. It is a common element in the universe and is estimated at seventh in total abundance in the Milky Way and the Solar System. Bryson, who I quoted earlier, points out that when we take a breath, the air we take in consists of eighty percent Nitrogen. However, as Bryson goes on to explain: *"When you take a breath, the nitrogen in the air goes into your lungs and straight back out again."* This is because nitrogen does not interact with other elements, such as oxygen – which comes next.

OXYGEN – Oxygen is the Earth's most common element and is the third most abundant element in the universe. Any serious lack of oxygen and we would not be able to survive. What is intriguing about hydrogen and oxygen is that they are among the lightest of elements. However, combine the two in the scientific formula H_2O, two parts hydrogen and one part oxygen, and the result is water, a much heavier compound. Water, of course, is essential, given the fact that the human body consists of as much as 50% – 70% water.

PHOSPHORUS – Phosphorus is an element essential to the sustaining of life, largely through phosphates, compounds containing the phosphate ion, PO_4^{3-}. Phosphates are a component of DNA, RNA, ATP and phospholipids, complex compounds fundamental to cells. Elemental phosphorus was first isolated from human urine, and bone ash was an important early phosphate source. Phosphate mines contain fossils because phosphate is present in the fossilized deposits of animal remains and excreta. Low phosphate levels are an important limit to growth in some aquatic systems. The vast majority of the phosphorus compounds which are mined are used as fertilisers. Other applications include organophosphorus compounds in detergents, pesticides and nerve agents.

The Royal Society of Chemistry which has identified these six elements, say that the atoms of five of them (H, O, C, P and N) when combined, form sugar phosphates that make up the back-bone polynucleotides of *'Deoxyribose Nucleic Acid'* (our DNA). Other combinations consist of Thyamine, Adenine, Cytosine and Guanine, the same making up the microscopic gene-carrying chromosomes in the nucleus of a human cell.

Of the 0.90% of our bodies which are made up of other elements, these include Cobalt, Chlorine, Chromium, Copper, Manganese, Molybdenum, Potassium, Sodium, Sulphur, Tin and Vanadium.

Some of these sub-elements are microscopic, for example, approximately twenty atoms of Cobalt, but without them our bodies would be incomplete and unable to survive.

Space – or continued concentration! – does not permit for a detailed summary of all of these sub-elements, but I would like to point out the importance of one of them: Potassium.

POTASSIUM – Potassium ions are vital for the functioning of all living cells. The transfer of potassium ions across nerve cell membranes is necessary for normal nerve transmission. Potassium deficiency and excess can result in a number of physical symptoms, including ectopic heartbeats and other electrocardiographic abnormalities. Vegetables and fruit are well-known to be good dietary sources of potassium.

For evolution to be remotely plausible, it would have needed the right proportion of the six basic elements, plus the 0.90% of the other elements, for the human genome – the complete set of DNA instructions in a living cell which are distributed among our chromosomes – for them to combine in order for men and women to be formed. Thus to believe in evolution requires much more faith than it does to believe in Creation!

DOMESTIC DUST

In his first letter to the church in Corinth, Paul refers to dust as he links Adam the first man, with Jesus the Son of Man and the Lord of Heaven and Earth. Paul's teaching is that if we who are like Adam are made of dust, we may, if we aspire to, become like Jesus. Or as Athanasius wisely concluded:

"He became like us that we might become like Him."

In this letter, (1 Corinthians 15:47–49) Paul wrote of those who had not been redeemed – those who had not believed in Jesus – and those who had been redeemed.

> *The first man* [Adam] *was of the earth, made of dust; the second Man* [Jesus] *is the Lord from heaven. As was the*

man of dust, so also are those who are made of dust; and as is the heavenly Man, so also are those who are heavenly. And as we have borne the image of the man of dust [Adam], *we shall also bear the image of the heavenly Man* [Jesus].

Of man's opinion of himself, it was the Preacher who said: *"Vanity of vanities, all is vanity."* (Ecclesiastes 1:2). And in 1613, Sir Thomas Overbury added: *"Beauty is only skin deep!"*

So what is it about our skin? Skin is the body's largest organ and consists of seven layers. Skin is part of the body's innate immune system and acts as the first barrier against germs, ultraviolet light, chemicals and injury. Skin helps to maintain the body's temperature and prevent water loss. Over time skin cells become detached and this is why much of the material taken up by vacuum cleaners is skin, or dust! What happens to our skin is also a reminder of how God can change people's lives. In Paul's second letter to the Church in Corinth, Paul wrote to encourage its ageing populace:

Therefore we do not lose heart. Even though our outward man is perishing [the ageing process!], *yet the inward man is being renewed day by day.* (2 Corinthians 4:16).

Psalm 22, which is prophetic – as are others of David's Psalms – details Jesus' birth to be followed by His death when He reached the end of His earth-bound mission.

"But You are He who took Me out of the womb; You made Me trust while on My mother's breasts. I was cast upon You from birth, from My mother's womb You have been My God." (verses 9–10). Then when He was dying: *"My strength is dried up like a potsherd, and My tongue clings to My jaws; You have brought Me to the **dust** of death."* (verse 15). *"All those who go down to the **dust** shall bow before Him. Even he who cannot keep himself alive."* (verse 29).

THE MASTER CRAFTSMAN

It is probably true for most Christians that their most well-known and much-loved statement in the Bible is John 3:16.

"For God so loved the world that He gave His only begotten Son, that whoever believes in Him should not perish but have everlasting life."

These words, of course, are words spoken by Jesus, and they describe God's loving-kindness for those He has created in His image. But when and why did God decide to send His Son into the world – perhaps the most important decision He has ever made? Was it when Mary, Jesus' mother, became pregnant? Or was it when Isaiah prophesied:

"Therefore the Lord Himself will give you a sign: Behold, the virgin shall conceive and bear a Son, and shall call His name Immanuel" – meaning: *'God-with-us'*. (Isaiah 7:14).

Or was it much earlier than this – before Isaiah lived?

The complete answer is there is much information within the Old Testament Scriptures – the Scriptures that Jesus so often referred to – and the New Testament Scriptures, which point to the when and the why God made His decision.

The apostle Peter, a close confidant of the Lord Jesus and in his first epistle, states we are not redeemed with corruptible things, like silver or gold, from our aimless conduct...

...but with the precious blood of Christ, as of a lamb without blemish and without spot. [The *'Lamb'* is a Passover Lamb].

Peter continues by testifying...

> ...*He indeed* [that is Jesus] *was foreordained **before the foundation of the world**, but was manifest in these last times for you...* (1 Peter 1:18-20).

At the time He was *'foreordained'*, was Jesus expected to be born as a Man before a man and his wife were created? If so, then the decision for His birth must have been taken before...

> ...*the LORD saw that the wickedness of man was great in the earth, and that every intent of the thoughts of his heart was only evil continually.* (Genesis 6:5).

Paul also asserts what his contemporary Peter wrote. In his letter to the new believers in Ephesus, Paul informs them that they have been chosen by God...

> ...*who has blessed us with every spiritual blessing in the heavenly places in Christ, **just as He chose us in Him before the foundation of the world**.* (Ephesians 1:3-4a).

Paul then adds to his thesis when writing to Titus – who he describes as *'...a true son in our common faith'*. Paul states that by the *'...acknowledgment of the truth'*, God's elect are...

> ...**in hope of eternal life, which God, who cannot lie, promised before time began.** (See Titus 1:1-4).

From these acknowledgments, and others such as what the writer of Hebrews (Hebrews 1:1-2) once wrote:

> *God, who at various times and in various ways spoke in time past to the fathers by the prophets, has in these last days spoken to us by His Son, whom He has appointed heir of all things, **through whom also He made the worlds**...*

...then it is entirely feasible that a thorough search of the Scriptures will affirm that God's Plan to send His Son into the world, pre-dates what took place during the first Seven Days. If such a decision and timing is likely, then the first account of Creation may have more to do with God's Son, the Lord Jesus, than it has to do with Adam and his wife Eve.

The Rev. Adolph Saphir (1831 – 1891), a Hungarian Jew who converted to Christianity and became a Jewish Presbyterian missionary, wrote in his book CHRIST AND THE SCRIPTURES...

For He is the centre and kernel of the inspired record. The history of Jesus does not begin with His birth in Bethlehem.

In this study, my aim is to show how I see Jesus as being the focus of the Bible from its beginning to its end. In the New Testament, Jesus is seen as being the Saviour of those who put their faith and trust in Him, but in the Old Testament, Jesus, although referred to many times, in the main He is the subject of prophecy. It is essential therefore to consider both sections; the section that was written before Jesus was born, and the section that was written after He had died, rose from the dead, and then ascended to return to His Father.

BREAD AND WINE

Shortly before Jesus was arrested then taken to face a mock trial before being led out of Jerusalem to be crucified, Jesus took bread, gave it to His disciples, then said to them:

"Take, eat; this is My body."

The bread Jesus gave to His disciples was a representative token of Himself – His physical body.

Jesus then took a cup filled with red wine and said to them:

"Drink from it, all of you. For this is My blood of the new covenant, which is shed for many for the remission of sins." (See Matthew 26:26-28).

The cup of wine Jesus gave to His disciples represented His blood, His *'Fount of Life'* which was poured out when He was nailed to a Roman cruciform. It is in these two elements, the physical body of Jesus and His blood, that we can receive forgiveness for our sin and God's assurance of eternal life. What Jesus suffered at Calvary is that it was anticipated before men and women were made in God's image, and before they sinned against Him. When Paul wrote to the Colossians about Jesus, he described his Saviour as being:

*He is the image of the invisible God, the firstborn over all creation. For by Him **all things** were created that are in heaven and that are on the earth, visible and invisible, whether thrones or dominions or principalities or powers. **All things** were created through Him and for Him. And He is before **all things**, and in Him **all things** consist.* (Colossians 1:15-17).

In the above summary of what Paul describes as *'All Things'*, Paul refers to the Master Craftsman who, when His work on Earth was completed – having achieved *'All Things'* that were written about Him – confirmed it with His personal oath:

"It is finished!" (John 19:30).

Jesus' epitaph is a parallel of when God *'Finished'* His work of Creation. The next day, *'...on the seventh day God ended His work ... and He rested on the seventh day'.* (Genesis 2:2).

In the book of Isaiah, Isaiah describes the betrothal of the Lamb of God who came to bring to full commitment, a Bride prepared and made ready for God's Kingdom.

*The LORD of Hosts will make on this **mount** for all the peoples a banquet of rich viands* [food imperative for life] *a banquet of choice wines – of rich viands seasoned with marrow, of choice wines well refined. And He will destroy on this **mount** the shroud that is drawn over the faces of all the peoples and the covering that is spread over all the nations: He will destroy death forever. My Lord GOD will wipe the tears away from all faces and will put an end to the reproach of His people over all the earth – for it is the LORD who has spoken. In that day they shall say: "This is our God, we trusted in Him, and He delivered us. This is the LORD, in whom we trusted; let us rejoice and exalt in His deliverance!"* (Isaiah 25:6–9). This **'Mount'** is Calvary. (These verses are quoted from the Jewish Study Bible).

Concerning this prophecy, the renowned and prolific Bible commentator, Matthew Henry, (1662–1714), wrote:

We have here [Isaiah 25:6–9] a prophecy of the salvation and grace brought unto us by Jesus Christ, into which the prophets enquired and searched diligently.

In tandem with Isaiah's prophecy, in John 6:55 we recall what Jesus said concerning two of His personal attributes.

"For My flesh is food indeed, and My blood is drink indeed."

This altruistic statement by Jesus is not only linked to Isaiah 25:6 (*'Rich Viands and Choice Wine'*), it is also linked to Proverbs 9:1–6 and how the writer of Proverbs describes God's Kingdom and its Seven Pillars of Wisdom. The first two Pillars are a citation of what has been provided for men and women in the body and blood (the Person) of God's Son.

1, **Rich Viands**. Food that is essential for life itself and is symbolic of the life-giving potential of Jesus' body.

2. **Choice Wine.** Wine that is symbolic of Jesus' blood.

The provision of His body and His blood was seen when Jesus turned water in six earthen vessels (Six the numeric as a token of His physical body) into wine (Wine a token of His blood; His life). The Master of the wedding feast said to Him:

"You have kept the good wine [the choice wine] *until now!"* (John 2:10).

That which follows in this study is a description of what has been for millennia, God's Plan of salvation for those He has created and who have responded positively and in faith to His invitation. God's Plan has been designed for those who would choose Jesus to be their Saviour and Lord and who would one day attend His marriage supper. However, is attendance at His banquet by invitation only? The answer is *"YES"*. The *'GOOD NEWS'* is: Everyone is invited.

GOD'S HOUSE

Pillars are accredited with their primary purpose – they give support and strength to the structure(s) for which they have been designed. Such pillars are the focus of Proverbs 9:1-6.

Wisdom has built her house, she has hewn out her seven pillars. (Proverbs 9:1).

This House – God's House – planned for since the beginning of time for those who believe in God, is the house/home where they will one day be gathered together to be with Himself and with His Son; He who is the Master Craftsman. His disciple Peter also refers to the Master Craftsman.

Coming to Him [Jesus] *as to a living stone, rejected indeed by men, but chosen by God and precious.* (1 Peter 2:4).

God's House, founded on this *'Living Stone'* and its Seven Pillars of Wisdom, is precious, for it has been designed and called into being for those who accept Wisdom's advice.

Listed in Proverbs 9:1-6, the Seven Pillars of Wisdom are for those whose yearning is for God and whose chosen priority is to: *"Get wisdom! Get understanding!"* (Proverbs 4:5).

1. WISDOM – **'She has slaughtered her meat.'** *'For He [that is Jesus] was cut off from the land of the living.'* (Isaiah 53:8).

2. WISDOM – **'She has mixed her wine.'** *'God was in Christ reconciling the world to Himself.'* (2 Corinthians 5:19).

3. WISDOM – **'She has also furnished her table.'** *"You prepare a table before me..."* (Psalm 23:5).

4. WISDOM – **'She cries out from the highest places of the city, "Whoever is simple, let him turn in here!"'** Jesus said to His disciples: *"...and you shall be witnesses to Me in [the city of] Jerusalem and Judea..."* (Acts 1:8).

5. WISDOM – includes: **'...him who lacks understanding.'** As well as Jerusalem and Judea, Jesus then added those: *"...in Samaria and to the end of the earth."* (Acts 1:8).

6. WISDOM – **"Come, eat of my bread and drink of the wine I have mixed."** Taking a portion of bread, Jesus said to His followers: *"Take, eat; this is My body."* He then took a cup of wine, saying: *"This is My blood of the new covenant which is shed for many.* (Mark 14:22-25).

7. WISDOM – **"Forsake foolishness and live, and go in the way of understanding."** *"Today, if you will hear His voice, do not harden your hearts."* (Hebrews 4:7).

Given that world-wide invitations have been issued to Jews and to Gentiles to attend the Lord's marriage supper at His table is the core purpose for these Seven Pillars of Wisdom, should not be taken lightly. And also the synoptic sequence of these Seven Pillars is to see them with equal importance. When cautioning those who did not believe in God and in His Son the Lord Jesus, the apostle Paul – who saw himself as a *'Bondservant of Jesus Christ'* (Romans 1:1) – wrote:

> *For since the creation of the world His* [that is God's] *invisible attributes are clearly seen, being understood by the things that are made, even His eternal power and Godhead, so that they are without excuse.* (Romans 1:20).

Notice that in His letter to the Church in Rome, Paul refers to *'The Creation of the World'*. For Paul, Creation was a subject for which there was no contest.

The authors Craig G. Bartholomew and Ryan P. O'Dowd have explained for their readers in their theological introduction to OLD TESTAMENT WISDOM LITERATURE, the importance of wine, bread and oil.

> Wine, together with bread and oil, are the most symbolic of foods. As Leon Kass argues, eating is perhaps the most powerful act we do as physical creatures. Compared to wisdom, eating may be a humble subject, but is no trivial matter. It is the first and most urgent activity of all animal and human life. We are only because we eat. Food [they point out] reminds us of our dependence as creatures, and wine of the mystery and richness of Creation.

> In the New Testament, with the arrival of the Messiah, the Kingdom and the Lord's Supper [See John 6:53–58], bread, wine and oil (the Holy Spirit), feature centrally as we feast on the Lord himself as our entrance into the redeemed

human life. These foods stand as signs against the evil, injustice and poverty in the world, while also affirming the place of celebration.

Such a basic and yet profound assessment by Bartholomew and O'Dowd of what is referred to in Proverbs, is but a summary of what took place at the last meal Jesus presided over with His disciples – and only a matter of a few hours before He died by crucifixion.

This meal, a facsimile of what is to come, is to be repeated when for those who will be in attendance at the *'Lord's Supper'* – the *'Last Supper'* being a preamble – so long as they have responded positively to His invitation, will be able to rejoice and give thanks to God for His love and His mercy.

In designing the role of the Seven Pillars of Wisdom and the other two aspects of My Master's Sevenfold Plan, I thought to recall some of the words that Jesus shared with His disciples soon after He had been raised from the dead. I suspect His disciples may have been confused, aware that their Master had been crucified on a tree and that He had died and been buried in a garden tomb – which had then been sealed by a large stone. (Remember the large stone which Joshua had placed under an oak tree that was by the LORD's Sanctuary, and which had heard all of the LORD's words to His people).

So what did His Disciples make of His resurrection? And also, who was it who moved the large stone?

During His time with His disciples, Jesus frequently quoted from Scripture (the Old Testament) about Himself. After He was raised from the dead, He continued to recall that which the prophets had written about Him. The following is what Luke wrote concerning what Jesus said to His disciples about Him being the fulfilment of prophecy.

"These are the words which I spoke to you while I was still with you, that all things must be fulfilled which were written in the Law of Moses and the Prophets and the Psalms concerning Me." (Luke 24:44).

In willing His disciples to understand, Jesus explained that those who had written about Him much earlier, men such as Moses, David and Isaiah; that they had done so because they had been inspired and led by the Holy Spirit.

For His disciples, these Old Testament Scriptures were what they were to depend on when assuring others that Jesus, the Christ their Messiah, was the Saviour of the world.

Today with the virtual absence of real assurance that billions are facing in their daily lives – less so for those who have received Jesus into their lives – His followers are beginning to consider: *"Is His Second Coming, coming soon?"* In the first chapter of the book of Revelation it is stated:

> **Behold, He is coming with clouds, and every eye will see Him, even they who pierced Him. And all the tribes of the earth will mourn because of Him. Even so, Amen. "I am the Alpha and the Omega, the Beginning and the End," says the Lord, "who is and who was and who is to come, the Almighty."** (Revelation 1:7–8).

When God's Son's Second Coming is implemented, physically and for the first time in human history, it may be possible via Social Media for all to witness at the same time His next appearance. If so, the prophecy: *'Every eye will see Him'* will be fulfilled. His Second Coming will be the Omega – The End. The Alpha – The Beginning – is the when and why the book of Genesis was written. Welcome to PART TWO.

****

PART TWO

THE FIRST DAY, THE FIRST APPOINTED TIME OF THE LORD, THE FIRST PILLAR OF WISDOM

In the beginning God created the heavens and the earth. The earth was without form, and void; and darkness was on the face of the deep. And the Spirit of God was hovering over the face of the waters. Then God said: "Let there be light"; and there was light. And God saw the light, that it was good; and God divided the light from the darkness. God called the light Day, and the darkness He called Night. So the evening and the morning were the first day. (Genesis 1:1–5).

The first five verses of the Bible embrace the commencement of my Master's Sevenfold Plan. Given what is said about the First Day, is it as straightforward as many have assumed it to be? Let us take God's first command: *"Let there be light"* – which He then called *"Day"*. Clearly this light is not the light of the Sun for the Sun does not feature until the Fourth Day. Is it possible the reason why God called the light **"Day"**, is in what we saw earlier in Luke chapter one (page 27), how Jesus is described as: *"The **Dayspring** from on high... ...to give **light** to those who sit in darkness and the shadow of death."* ? This takes us on to what was later made known to the apostle John, and is in keeping with the First Day. The following is taken from the penultimate chapter of the Bible.

*Now I saw a **new heaven and a new earth** ... the holy city, New Jerusalem, coming down out of heaven from God, prepared as a bride adorned for her husband. ... The city* *had no need of the sun or of the moon to shine in it, for the glory of God illuminated it.* **The Lamb is its light.** *(There shall be no night there).* (Revelation 21:1-2 & 23 & 25b).

Again, the 'Lamb' who is the 'New Earth's Light', is Jesus.

Before the children of Israel were set-free from being slaves to the Egyptians, God told Moses to say to them that on the tenth day of the first Lunar month, they were to select one-year-old male lambs without blemish. Four days later, the preparation day for God's 'Pass-Over', the lambs were killed and blood from them was then painted on the doorposts and the door's lintel (crossbeam) of their houses as a sign their homes were occupied by God's people. (Exodus 12:1-13).

A few hours later, on the fifteenth day of the first month and at midnight (Exodus 12:29), a time of darkness (though there would have been a full Moon for Passover was timed to take place mid-way through the first Lunar month), God passed-over Egypt. For the children of Israel whose homes had been marked with blood from the Passover lambs, they were spared God's judgement. Thus nobody died. However, in the homes of the Egyptians whose door frames had *not* been painted with blood, all the first-born of the Egyptians died.

Let us now fast-forward 3,500 years. Janet and I, we live in a cul-de-sac where there are no street lights. When we are expecting visits from friends or family during the hours of darkness, to help them find their way to our home, we switch on an outside light that is next to our front door. To paint the doorposts and the door's lintel red would never occur to me.

But this is what God told the children of Israel to do – but not to use paint; instead to use the blood of a lamb. Why did God not instruct Moses to tell the children of Israel to mark their homes with lights; such as candles or oil lamps? Why blood?

And how was God able to see where they were in the dark? Is God's vision limited in the way our vision is limited? Or does God have the ability to see what we cannot see? For example, does God have *'Night Vision'*, or *'Infra-**Red** Vision'* that enabled Him to see the blood of the lambs in the dark?

Having prayed to God for their deliverance from slavery, the children of Israel were about to be granted their freedom. The instruction which God gave to them was that they were to select a one year-old male lamb, or a goat, and kill it on the fourteenth day of the first month in their Lunar Calendar. Next, God said to Moses and to his brother Aaron:

> *"And they shall take some of the blood and put it on the two doorposts and on the lintel of the houses where they eat it. Then they shall eat the flesh on that night; roasted in fire, with unleavened bread and with bitter herbs they shall eat it." ... "And thus you shall eat it: with a belt on your waist, your sandals on your feet, and your staff in your hand. So you shall eat it in haste. It is the LORD's Passover."* (Exodus 12:7, 8 & 11).

Now a certain conundrum arises in that having done as God had commanded – marked their houses so that God would be able to see the blood and where they were seeking shelter and protection – God then informed Moses that He would be: *"Passing-Over"* their homes at midnight. Why at midnight?

It appears God chose the darkest moment of the night to set in motion His people's freedom. Why did God do this, to select a time when it would have been very difficult for any person (but not God) to see and to distinguish the houses which had been marked with the lamb's blood, from those which had not? The clearest answer is in what we can learn from the events that took place in Jerusalem approximately one thousand five hundred years later.

The lamb's blood the people applied to the wooden crosspieces and uprights of their door frames; was representative of Jesus' blood when He was nailed to a cross of wood at Calvary. Having been appointed for death in this way, Jesus became the fulfilment of the Passover sacrifice – The Lamb of God who would set people free from their slavery to those things which can captivate, dominate and darken their lives.

THE EFFICACY OF JESUS' BLOOD

For those who may not be familiar with the Bible, it may be baffling why its many writers place so much emphasis on blood. For example, Jesus' blood is referred to many more times than His death. In order for Jesus to replicate the profile of a Passover blood sacrifice, it follows that Jesus had to array Himself with His own flesh and blood. It would have circumvented God's Plan if He had not done so. The reason Jesus took on flesh and blood was to set us free; then to help us overcome the vagaries of temptation. This is why there are truths about the efficacy of His blood we need to explore.

The first is that blood contains oxygen. Oxygen is odourless, tasteless, colourless, and most important of all, it is *FREE!* Without blood and oxygen there can be no life. Because oxygen is *FREE*, it is a reminder of what Paul wrote.

> *For the wages of sin is death, but the **free** gift of God is eternal life in Christ Jesus our Lord.* (Romans 6:23).

Given that life and its choices apply to us all, the seriousness of choice is in what Moses once said to the children of Israel.

> *"I call heaven and earth as witnesses today against you, that I have set before you life and death, blessings and cursing; therefore choose life, that both you and your descendants may live."* (Deuteronomy 30:19).

Listed in the Bible are three injunctions about our myriad of blood vessels in which there is life. This life consists of blood cells plus oxygen. Blood cells are formed in the soft spongy material that is present in the centre of our bones. Oxygen – which we are in need of constantly and has been made *freely* available from the trees and plants – is God's creative genius. Without a constant supply of oxygen there can be no life. In the following three injunctions it is God who is speaking.

1. *"But you shall not eat flesh with its life, that is, **its blood**."* (Genesis 9:4).

2. *"**For the life of the flesh is in the blood**, and I have given it to you upon the altar to make atonement for your souls; for it is the **blood** that makes atonement for the soul."* (Leviticus 17:11).

3. *"Only be sure that you do not eat the blood, **for the blood is the life**; you may not eat the life with the meat. You shall not eat it; you shall pour it on the earth like water. You shall not eat it, that it may go well with you and your children after you, when you do what is right in the sight of the LORD."* (Deuteronomy 12:23–25).

According to National Geographic, approximately seventy percent of the oxygen which the natural world produces daily arises from marine plants and plant-like organisms. Ocean-living plants release molecular oxygen as a waste product of photosynthesis (as do the majority of plants).

In photosynthesis, plants capture **'Sun-Light'** and use its energy to split carbon dioxide and water, making sugar for itself and releasing oxygen as a by-product. The dominance of marine life as the main oxygen producer makes perfect sense when you consider that seventy percent of our planet's surface area is taken up by the Seven Seas.

The reason I've combined our need for oxygen with blood, is because of the method used to bring about the death of Jesus. Pierre Barbet, who has studied crucifixion, points out that asphyxiation results from the way the victim dies with the weight of the body suspended by the out-stretched arms.

Barbet's recalling of the asphyxiation of Jesus – leading to His deoxygenated blood which is known as 'Venous Blood' – is that death would be an inevitable consequence because of the hyper-expansion of His chest muscles and lungs.

In the design and rhythmical ordering of our blood supply system, there are three truths we need to grasp if we are to fully understand the efficacy of the blood of Jesus.

1. There are Seven Facets to blood. They are Antibodies, Electrolytes, Heat, Hormones, Nourishment, Oxygen, and Vitamins. In the Book of Common Prayer, we are instructed by faith to: *"...feed on Jesus in our hearts."*

2. To assist (via the Spleen) in the filtering and removal of damaged and worn-out blood cells. Cleansing is the method by which Jesus' blood is so highly effective.

3. To trace, identify and eradicate pathogens which can cause harm. This is done by white blood cells which have an important role to play in fighting bacterial, viral, fungal and parasitic infections. The cleansing of our internal organs is probably the second most important function of blood. White blood cells also help to heal wounds and taking in matter – such as dead cells, tissue debris and discarded red blood cells. They are our constant protection from foreign bodies that enter our blood-stream, such as allergens. White blood cells also help to protect against mutated cells, such as cancer.

Having considered the life properties of blood and our needs, particularly blood's cleansing ability, we can now see why the writer to the Hebrews describes how the blood of Jesus sanctifies (makes holy) in cleansing us from our sin.*

But Christ came as High Priest of the good things to come, with the greater and more perfect tabernacle not made with hands that is, not of this creation. Not with the blood of goats and calves, but with His own blood He entered the Most Holy Place once for all, having obtained eternal redemption.

For if the blood of bulls and goats and the ashes of a heifer, sprinkling the unclean, sanctifies for the purifying of the flesh, how much more shall the blood of Christ, who through the eternal Spirit offered Himself without spot [blemish] *to God, cleanse your conscience from dead works to serve the living God?* (Hebrew 9:11 – 14).

The above is the raison d'être that Jesus' blood can have in our lives; in a substitutional and in a metaphorical sense.

Turning to the continuous flow of blood through the myriads of our blood vessels, it is widely known that without this blood supply, life would be impossible. Injure a main artery and permit a rapid escape of blood, unless swiftly stemmed, death can take place in a matter of minutes. Such a rupture of an arterial blood vessel can happen internally – and also from an external influence. When Jesus, our Passover Lamb, was crucified and died, due mainly to a lack of oxygen, His side was then pierced and His blood was poured out upon the earth like water. (Note again, Deuteronomy 12:20–28).

---

* I acknowledge guidance provided for this appraisal of Jesus' blood from Alan Stibbs' (1901–1971) book, HIS BLOOD WORKS.

This, therefore, as the apostle Paul instructs his converts:

> *Beware lest anyone cheat you through philosophy and empty deceit, according to the tradition of men, according to the basic principles of the world, and not according to Christ. For in Him dwells all the fullness of the Godhead bodily; and you are **complete in Him**, who is the head of all principality and power.* (Colossians 2:8-10).

How can it be that we can be complete in Jesus: *'Complete in Him'*? It is because Jesus, the Son of God, and having become like one of us through His physical birth, by His suffering and His dying, that His life which was in His blood was poured out at Calvary. Consequently, by His blood:

> *He who has the Son has life; he who does not have the Son of God does not have life.* (1 John 5:12).

Having studied the Hebrew writings, Paul understood these truths, and so he provided a résumé of God's Sevenfold Plan.

> *For our citizenship is in heaven, from which we also eagerly wait for the Saviour, the Lord Jesus Christ, who will transform our lowly body, that it may be conformed to His glorious body, according to the working by which He is able even to subdue all things to Himself.* (Philippians 3:20-21).

JESUS THE LIGHT OF THE WORLD AND THE PASSOVER LAMB

Having considered the basics, it now appears the *'light'* that is spoken of on the First Day (Genesis 1:3), and the lambs that were slain on the First Appointed Time of the LORD – Passover – that these two events were intended to portray to all of mankind an authentic representation of Jesus. They are illustrations, or pictures. Jesus is for us not only the *'Light of the World'*, He is the *'Passover Lamb'* who died at Calvary.

This is how and why these two ancient Biblical events are associated: The *'light'* that appeared on the First Day, and the Jewish Feast of *'Passover'*. What God did for the children of Israel when He *'Passed-Over'* Egypt to set His people free at the time of the Passover, was then repeated when His Son, the Lord Jesus, died on the cross at Calvary.

For believers, *'Our being in Christ Jesus'* means that *'Light'* can indeed shine in a dark place – in our hearts and our thoughts. This, I believe, was what God intended when He passed-over Egypt. God was looking to the time when His Son would surrender His *'life'* in order for us to know freedom from sin.

When Jesus arrived in Bethany on the tenth day of the first month (John 12:1) – *The same day as in the days of Moses when the Passover lambs were chosen for the Passover and the people's evening meal* – it was because, four days later, on the eve of the remembrance of Passover, Jesus was to die as He became *'The Lamb of God'* to set free from their slavery and bondage to sin, those who put their faith and trust in Him.

The night before Jesus was crucified – and in the hearing of His disciples – Jesus prayed to His Father. The following two statements were included in the words Jesus prayed.

> 1, *"And now, O Father, glorify Me together with Yourself, with the glory which I had with You **before** the world was."*

> 2, *"...for You loved Me **before** the foundation of the world."* (John 17:5 & 24b).

Recalling how Jesus is *'The Light of the World'* and how on the First Day God had said: *"Let there be light"*, the evening before the *'Light of the World'* was about to be extinguished at the time of Passover, Jesus let it be known to His disciples what was about to take place. Thus He said to them:

> *"A little while longer the **light** is with you. Walk while you have the **light**, lest darkness overtake you; he who walks in darkness does not know where he is going. While you have the **light**, believe in the **light**, that you may become sons of **light**."* (John 12:35-36).

Earlier, Jesus had also informed His disciples:

> **"I am the light of the world. He who follows Me shall not walk in darkness but have the light of life."** (John 8:12).

Jesus, therefore, the *'Light of the World'*, is linked to the First Day when God said: *"Let there be light"*, and the first Jewish Feast, Passover – the day when the children of Israel were set-free at midnight from what was their darkest hour. The time when the Jewish people would have been preparing for their celebratory Passover meal, was the chosen and correct time for Jesus to have taken His last breath.

The first appearance of *'Light'* confirms how Jesus became *'...the Lamb slain from the foundation of the world.'* (Revelation 13:8). i.e., On the First Day. It was that He might take upon Himself the darkness of our sin. And so the death of Jesus at the timing of the Passover observance, is tied unquestionably to the First Pillar of Wisdom:

> **'She has slaughtered her meat'.** (Proverbs 9:2).

Is it not highly noteworthy how the First Pillar of Wisdom's description of how Jesus was to die is so harsh and so cruel? Yet it is also repeated prophetically by God's servant, Isaiah.

> *He was oppressed and He was afflicted yet He opened not His mouth; He was led as a lamb to the **slaughter**, and as a sheep before its shearers is silent, so He opened not His mouth.* (Isaiah 53:7).

In Hebrew, the word used for altar (*Mizbeach*) is connected to the terms: *'To slaughter and/or to sacrifice'*. To enable us to be set-free from our sin, Jesus knew He had to die and in accordance with the assertion of the First Pillar of Wisdom.

The *'light'* which God announced on the First Day, was made known before the measurement of Earth's time began, then later, at the time of Passover, God's *'Light'* was extinguished.

Is this the reason why when Jesus was dying, the Sun's light, the Sun's radiance, was withheld from noon for three hours? (Luke 23:44). If this reasoning is for real (and I stress this is my own conclusion as I have not encountered it previously), then it is confirmed in what God inspired His servant Amos to announce.

> *"And it shall come to pass in that day," says the Lord God, "That I will make the sun go down at noon, and I will darken the earth in broad daylight; I will turn your feasts* [including Passover] *into mourning, and all your songs into lamentation ... I will make it like mourning for an only son, and its end like a bitter day."* (Amos 8:9–10).

This prophecy explains how the first of the Seven Appointed Times of the LORD, Passover, is linked to the First Day and the First Pillar of Wisdom: **'She has slaughtered her meat'**.

In his book, JESUS THE JEWISH THEOLOGIAN, Dr. Brad Young refers to Proverbs 3:19 – *'The LORD by wisdom founded the earth...'* Dr. Young then refers to Proverbs 9:1 – *'Wisdom has built her house, she has hewn out her seven pillars.'* In his conclusion about this brief communiqué, Dr. Young states his own conviction about my Master's Seven Pillars of Wisdom.

"These seven pillars refer to the seven days in which God created the World."

When I first began to consider this topic, I was not able to recall another suggesting how the Seven Days of Creation, which are listed in the first two chapters of the Bible, and the Seven Pillars of Wisdom (Proverbs 9:1-6), that they are in a definitive way connected with Jesus. It was not until much later that I read Dr. Young's book. However, by this time, my thoughts had already begun to crystallise around the fact that these two Biblical narratives are so similar.

Deliverance from ungodly temptations which can so easily become our task-masters and is the greatest danger we face, can only take place if there is a way of rescuing people. For Jewish people, they continue to recall this lesson when they celebrate the Hebrew Passover observance: The time when God rescued His people after four hundred years of slavery.

As we remember Jesus being the *'Light of the World'* and how He must have suffered at the time of Passover, Matthew reminds us of how Jesus fulfilled one of Isaiah's prophecies that speaks of the light and of how Jesus came to defeat the power of temptation and the consequences of sin (darkness).

> *And leaving Nazareth, He came and dwelt in Capernaum, which is by the sea, in the regions of Zebulun and Naphtali, that it might be fulfilled which was spoken by Isaiah the prophet saying: "The land of Zebulun and the land of Naphtali, by the way of the sea, beyond the Jordon, Galilee of the Gentiles; the people who sat in darkness have seen a great light, and upon those who sat in the region of the shadow of death, light has dawned."'* (Matthew 4:13-16).

The Scripture Matthew refers to can be found in Isaiah 9:1-2.

John the apostle, who portrays Jesus as being the Son of God, commences his gospel by using the same introduction that we find in Genesis: *'In the beginning...'* By the guidance of the

Holy Spirit, John then refers to the two agencies of light and darkness to explain why Jesus adopted a physical existence.

> *In the beginning was the Word* [Jesus], *and the Word was with God, and the Word was God. He was in the beginning with God.* All things were made through Him, and without Him nothing was made that was made. In Him was life, and the life was the light of men. And the light shines in the darkness and the darkness did not comprehend it."* (John 1:1– 5). ***** See Genesis 1:1

No surprise then that God is able to see in the dark. John's confirmation is a reminder of God's first command when He said: *"Let there be light."* John then continues by stating…

> *…the Word* [Logos] *became flesh* [A physical body] *and dwelt among us, and we beheld His glory.* (John 1:14).

John then introduces us to John the Baptist – whose name means: *'God's Favour'* – who, he says, came *'…to bear witness of the Light, that all through him might believe.'*

John stresses the fact that John the Baptist…

> *…was not that Light, but was sent to bear witness of that Light. That was the true Light* [the Lord Jesus] *which gives light to every man coming into the world.* (John 1:7–9).

Given that John wrote of the *'Light'* (Jesus, God's Son), was it because John was conversant with Proverbs? In Proverbs chapter eight, the writer recalls one of the most beautiful and compelling passages to be found in the Bible of the relationship between Jesus and His Father. This, His own witness, is a description of what took place *before* the First Day (whereas the account in Genesis 1:1–5 of the First Day was written for the benefit of others).

THE MASTER CRAFTSMAN - (Proverbs 8:22-31)

*"The LORD possessed me at the beginning of His way,
Before His works of old."*

*"I have been established from everlasting,
From the beginning, before there was ever an earth.
When there were no depths I was brought forth,
When there were no fountains abounding with water."*

*"Before the mountains were settled,
Before the hills, I was brought forth;
While as yet He had not made the earth or the fields,
Or the primal dust of the world."* [Note: 'The Primal Dust'].

*"When He prepared the heavens; I was there,
When He drew a circle on the face of the deep,
When He established the clouds above,
When He strengthened the fountains of the deep,
When He assigned to the sea its limit,
So that the waters would not transgress His command.
When He marked out the foundations of the earth,
Then I was beside Him as a master craftsman;
And I was daily His delight,
Rejoicing always before Him,
Rejoicing in His inhabited world,
And my delight was with the sons of men."*

Of this His enduring heritage – of the *'One'* who bore witness to these events – Charles Bridges (1794-1869), a leading Christian of his time and in 1846, wrote:

So glorious are the rays of eternal supreme Deity, distinct personality, and essential unity, that the mysterious, ever-blessed Being – *'The Word, who was in the beginning with God, and was God'* – now undoubtedly stands before us.

Curiously, to pry into the mode of His subsistence, would be intruding into those things which we have not seen. To receive His own revelation of Himself is our reverential privilege.

Seventy five years later (1921) Professor Gustaf Dalman D.D., Provost of the Church of the Redeemer in Jerusalem and who was conversant in Greek, Hebrew and Aramaic, published his book JESUS-JESCHUA. (In 1929, Reverend Paul P. Levertoff translated Dalman's book into English).

In his book Professor Dalman writes of the Master Craftsman plus three other character features of the Lord Jesus. The paragraphs I have selected and set-out below are taken from Professor Dalman's book.

Professor Gustaf Dalman writes:

Our Lord is addressed by Peter (Mark 9:5 & 11:21) and [twice] by the traitor [Judas] (Matthew 26:49 & Mark 14:45) as *'Rabbī'*, meaning: *'My great One'* – the usual designation of a *'Teacher'*, but also of a *'Master Craftsman'* and a *'Chief of Robbers'*. This can be Hebrew as well as Aramaic.

But Rabbūnī (= *Rabbbōnī*) with which the blind man in Jericho (Mark 10:51), and Mary Magdaline (John 20:16) addressed our Lord, is without doubt Aramaic. According to St John it would have to be translated with *'My Teacher'*. But it is in fact an intensified form of the usual *'Rabbī'*, which can only be rendered adequately [as] *'My Lord and Master'*.

In Jewish thought a Rabbī is an official who has had some experience of having possessed a trade. For Jesus, His trade was: '*...and the world was made through Him...*' (John 1:10).

Dalman's definition of a Rabbī – *'My Great One*, *'My Teacher'*, *'Master Craftsman'*, and *'Chief of robbers'* – was how those who recognised His trade-mark, came to believe in Jesus.

My Great One. Peter said to Jesus: *"Lord, to whom shall we go? You have the words of eternal life."* (John 6:68).

My Teacher. The people were amazed at His words, *'...for He taught them as one having authority'.* (Matthew 7:29).

Master Craftsman. *'When He marked out the foundations of the earth, then I was beside Him as a master craftsman; and I was daily His delight... '* (Proverbs 8:29b–30a).

Chief of Robbers. Don't be misled, Jesus was not a robber.

'Robber' is a term applied to those who rob from God. They fail to honour or respect Him. Jesus, my *Great One*, *Teacher*, *Master Craftsman* and *Chief of Robbers*, has taken on the task to forgive those who rob or take from God. So what did Jesus say when confronted by those sent out to arrest Him?

*In that hour Jesus said to the multitudes, "Have you come out, as against a **robber**, with swords and clubs to take Me? I sat daily with you, teaching in the temple, and you did not seize Me. But all this was done that the Scriptures of the prophets might be fulfilled."* (Matthew 26:55–56).

Later in His reply to one of two robbers who addressed Him as *"Lord"*, Jesus promised him: *"...today you will be with Me in Paradise."* (Luke 23:42–43). His assurance in His last hour to a robber who was about to die, is endorsed by the TALMUD. *"There are those who gain eternity in a lifetime, others who gain it in one brief hour."* For this particular robber, of the prophecies which related to Jesus before His death, the only one which remained outstanding was Isaiah 53:12.

So the Scripture was fulfilled which says, "And He was numbered with the transgressors [robbers]*."* (Mark 15:28).

For God to gift His Son to save men and women knowing how cruel they would treat and shame Him, was a commitment without precedent. And so as the apostle Paul wrote:

He who is the blessed and only Potentate [Sovereign]*, the King of kings and Lord of lords, who alone has immortality, dwelling in unapproachable light, whom no man has seen or can see, to whom be honor and everlasting power. Amen.* (1 Timothy 6:15–16).

In his letter to the new Church in Rome (Romans 13:12–14), Paul continues in like manner when he writes of the features of darkness and light. i.e., The events of the First Day.

Therefore let us cast off the works of darkness, and let us put on the armour of light. Let us walk properly, as in the day, not in revelry and drunkenness, not in lewdness and lust, not in strife and envy. But put on the Lord Jesus Christ, and make no provision for the flesh, to fulfil its lusts.

John the apostle also refers to these two opposites, light and darkness (or *'Merisms'*), in the first of his three letters. The following three paragraphs are taken from 1 John 1:5–10.

"This is the message which we have heard from Him and declare to you, that God is light and in Him is no darkness at all."

"If we say that we have fellowship with Him, and walk in darkness, we lie and do not practice the truth. But if we walk in the light as He is in the light, we have fellowship with one another and the blood of Jesus Christ His Son cleanses us from all sin."

"If we say that we have no sin, we deceive ourselves, and the truth is not in us. If we confess our sins, He is faithful and just to forgive us our sins and to cleanse us from all unrighteousness. If we say that we have not sinned, we make Him a liar, and His Word is not in us."

In summarising the First Day, *'Darkness'* replaced by *'Light'*; the First Appointed Time of the LORD, Passover; and the First Pillar of Wisdom, the death of Jesus; I have chosen what Jesus said when He explained to Nicodemus, God's Plan for those who were near to Him, and those who were afar off.

"For God did not send His Son into the world to condemn the world, but that the world through Him might be saved. He who believes in Him is not condemned, but he who does not believe is condemned already, because he has not believed in the name of the only begotten Son of God.

*And this is the condemnation, that the **light** has come into world, and men loved darkness rather **light**, because their deeds were evil. For everyone practicing evil hates the **light** and does not come to the **light**, lest his deeds should be exposed. But he who does the truth comes to the **light**, that his deeds may be clearly seen, that they have been done in God."* (John 3:17-21).

This is the second occasion Jesus has referred to the **'light'** five times. (John 12:35-36, page 54). Five equals *'GRACE'*. When the Bible speaks of Jesus as the **'light'**, it recalls that what happened to Jesus was a Merism of what happened on the First Day when the darkness was defeated by the light. And given that Jesus said that there is no condemnation for those who come to the **'Light'**, means that we can live in the light of His countenance (His Face). See Numbers 6:24-26.

****

THE SECOND DAY, THE SECOND APPOINTED TIME OF THE LORD, THE SECOND PILLAR OF WISDOM

Then God said, "Let there be a firmament in the midst of the waters, and let it divide the waters from the waters." Thus God made the firmament, and divided the waters which were under the firmament from the waters which were above the firmament; and it was so. And God called the firmament Heaven. So the evening and the morning were the second day. (Genesis 1:6–8).

Second in Creation's allocation is the division of water. For those who search the myriad of objects in the Universe, discovery of water is their main priority. At ninety-three million miles from the Sun, it is agreed by scientists that the Earth is the perfect distance from the Sun for water to exist and in its three forms – solid (ice), liquid and gas (vapour).

The acknowledgement by mariners of the waters that are below the expanse being divided from the waters above, is that sea water contains salt, and if they were to be cast-adrift in a lifeboat in the middle of an ocean they can still die of thirst. Though the lifeboat on its own may not save them, a quantity of desalinated (purified) drinking water may give them a few extra days and a greater chance of survival.

The water above the firmament refers to the hydrologic cycle that is powered by the Sun as sea water by evaporation turns to water vapour. And when the vapour condenses and forms clouds, the desalinated waters that are suspended within the clouds then fall on the land as rain. i.e., *'A New Creation'*.

According to the on-line encyclopedia Wikipedia, the Earth's unfailing water supply and cycle is the continual movement of water above, on, and below the surface of the Earth.

The mass of water on the Earth remains fairly constant over time, but the partitioning of the water into the major reservoirs of ice, fresh water, saline water and atmospheric water is variable, depending on a wide range of climatic changes. The water moves from one reservoir to another, for example from river to ocean, or from the oceans to the atmosphere, by the physical processes of evaporation, condensation, precipitation, infiltration, surface runoff and subsurface flow. In doing so, the water goes through three different states: solid, liquid and vapour.

The water cycle involves the exchange of energy that leads to temperature changes. As water evaporates, it takes up energy from its surroundings and cools the environment. When it condenses, it releases energy and warms the environment. These heat exchanges influence climate.

The evaporative phase of the cycle purifies water, which then replenishes the land with freshwater. The flow of liquid water and ice transports minerals across the globe.

It is also involved in reshaping the geological features of the Earth through processes which include soil erosion and sedimentation. The water cycle is also essential for the maintenance of most life and ecosystems on the planet.

It is in the evaporation phase of the Earth's water supply that water is purified. Only purified water is suitable for most plants and other land based forms of life to exist. For many, nature's process of purifying water is seemingly miraculous, yet it is happening constantly. And if for any climatic reason the rains should cease; critical situations can very soon arise.

When two is featured in the Bible, it can indicate separation, or division. In Ecclesiasticus we read: *'All things are double one against another; and He hath made nothing imperfect.'* (42:24). Derived from the Latin word *'Merismus'*, they are known as *'Merisms'*. Merisms are very common in the Bible and a well-known list is given by the Preacher – believed to be David's son Solomon – in Ecclesiastes 3:1–8.

To everything there is a season,
A time for every purpose under heaven:
A time to be born, and a time to die;
A time to plant, and a time to pluck what is planted;
A time to kill, and a time to heal;
A time to break down, and a time to build up;
A time to weep, and a time to laugh;
A time to mourn, and a time to dance;
A time to cast away stones, and a time to gather stones;
A time to embrace, and a time to refrain from embracing;
A time to gain, and a time to lose;
A time to keep, and a time to throw away;
A time to tear, and a time to sew;
A time to keep silence, and a time to speak;
A time to love, and a time to hate;
A time of war, and a time of peace.

It was on the Second Day God divided the waters by means of a firmament, which He then named: *"Heaven"*. Later Jesus taught His disciples that there is also a division between those who believe in God, and those who do not, and as a result there will always be two groups of people: the faithful who will go to *'Heaven'*, and unfaithful who will not.

Our freedom to choose life, or death, is linked to the way God divided the waters on the Second Day. And division is what Jewish people do when they observe their ancient festival of Unleavened Bread, when they remove all traces of leaven from their homes. When leaven is featured in the Bible, it is because spiritually, leaven can often be symbolic of sin.

In a similar way to what happens when a Chef adds yeast (leaven) to bread flour, sin can infiltrate, infuse and influence a person's life. Its point of access is wrong thoughts and desires, sight and pride. (1 John 2:16). See also Genesis 3:6. Yet for those who have been set-free from sin – i.e., they have been *'Born Again'* – no longer do their lives have to be influenced by habitual wrongdoing. Although all have sinned and fallen short of God's mark, the apostle Paul was able to say to the believers living in Corinth:

> *No temptation has overtaken you except such as is common to man; but God is faithful, who will not allow you to be tempted beyond what you are able, but with the temptation will also make the way of escape, that you may be able to bear it.* (1 Corinthians 10:13).

'Life and good', or *'Death and evil'*, (Deuteronomy 30:15) are enshrined in what God carried out on the Second Day when He established for all of mankind: the waters on the dry land (life), and the sea-waters (death). God's instructions for the Feast of Unleavened Bread – the Second Appointed Time – were given before the children of Israel had left Egypt. In Exodus, 12:16–17, we are told how God's people were to prepare themselves for their Second Feast of the LORD.

> *"On the first day there shall be a holy convocation, and on the seventh day there shall be a holy convocation for you. No manner of work shall be done on them; but that which everyone must eat – that only may be prepared by you. So you shall observe the Feast of Unleavened Bread, for on this same day I will have brought your armies out of the land of Egypt. Therefore you shall observe this day throughout your generations as an everlasting ordinance."*

Notice for the Feast of Unleavened Bread it is to be kept as an *'Everlasting Ordinance'*. The reason is because it marked the time when God's people left slavery behind in order to gain their promised freedom in the Promised Land.

The unleavened bread consumed at this Second Appointed Time is known as *'Matzah'*, and is perforated with its holes forming rows, or stripes. Matzah is a reminder of how the hands and feet of Jesus who was righteous, were perforated by nails. After He had died, like Adam, His side was opened with a spear and blood and water flowed from Him. (John 19:34). His release of blood and water – blood the primary source of life and water the building block of every living cell – is how our inner selves can be cleansed and refreshed.

In Psalm 22:16 (written approximately one thousand years before Jesus died), we read: *"They pierced My hands and My feet..."* And in Isaiah 53:5 (written about seven hundred years before Jesus died), we also read:

> *But He was wounded for our transgressions, He was bruised for our iniquities; the chastisement for our peace was upon Him, and by His stripes we are healed.*

The Second Feast, the act of dividing unleavened bread from what has become leavened, is linked to the act God carried out on the Second Day when He divided the waters – with the firmament in-between that He referred to as: *"Heaven"*.

Later God endorsed this same act when He divided the Red Sea to enable the children of Israel to leave Egypt after their four hundred years of slavery. (Genesis 15:13 & Acts 7:6).

These references to the division of water (the first occasion of the division of water is described in Genesis 1:6), are also references to the act of water baptism.

When a person who has come to faith in Jesus is baptised, in the act of baptism, the water is divided. Baptism, which is symbolic of dying, heralds the time when having passed from death to life, the baptised then becomes: 'A New Creation'. Baptism ratifies the life giving waters of the Second Day. And baptism (immersion in water) is an act that is not only carried out on behalf of believers. For millennia Jewish people have been immersing themselves in a 'Mikvah' – a type of bath – for them to seek and obtain religious purity.

For Jewish people, when they are immersed in the water, they pray and say in praise to God:

> "Barukh ata Adonai Elohenu melekh ha'olam asher kideshanu b'mitzvotav v'tzivanu al ha'tevillah."

This translates from the Hebrew into English as:

> "Blessed are You, O Lord, our God, King of the universe,
> Who has sanctified us with Your commandments
> And commanded us concerning the immersion."

In His Sermon on the Mount Jesus spoke of two gates. As we have seen, two can mean a division. i.e., 'A Merism'.

> "Enter by the narrow gate; for wide is the gate and broad is the way that leads to destruction, and there are many who go in by it. Because narrow is the gate and difficult is the way which leads to life, and there are few who find it." (Matthew 7:13–14).

The Second Day and the Second Jewish festival, the Feast of Unleavened Bread, they enable us to see how Jesus, who is righteous, died for the unrighteous. It was that He might bring us into a relationship with Himself and with His Father as a result of Him taking upon Himself the guilt of our sin.

Paul also knew about this aspect of division and of relating it to the nature of unleavened bread. In the first of his two letters to the members of the Church in Corinth, Paul wrote:

> *Do you not know that a little leaven leavens the whole lump? Therefore, purge out the old leaven, that you may be a new lump, since you truly are unleavened. For indeed Christ, our Passover, was sacrificed for us. Therefore let us keep the feast, not with the old leaven, nor with the leaven of malice and wickedness, but with the unleavened bread of sincerity and truth.* (1 Corinthians 5:6–8).

By using the metaphors of leavened and unleavened bread, Paul uses these symbols to explain how that when Jesus died, He enabled us to be cleansed from our sin and for our lives to be changed to lives of righteousness and holiness. Because Jesus was without sin, He is the embodiment of the Second Day and the Second Feast – the Feast of Unleavened Bread.

On one occasion when He outlined His destiny, Jesus said:

> *"I am the bread of life. He who comes to Me shall never hunger, and he who believes in Me shall never thirst."* (John 6:35).

Originating from the Second Feast and the overall Biblical creed, I believe Jesus may have been referring to the nature of unleavened bread, rather than leavened bread.

During His trial, Pilate, the leading authority in Jerusalem, questioned Jesus in a similar way as the Jewish priests would have examined the Passover lambs (*'Paschal Lambs'*) for any defects prior to sanctioning their deaths. Three times Pilate said of Jesus: *"I find no fault in Him."* (John 18:38 & 19:4 & 6). The reason was because Jesus was sinless. Both legally and morally, His execution was a travesty of human justice.

When Jesus attended a wedding festival to be told there was no **wine**, His mother said to the servants: *"Whatever He says to you, do it."* Jesus then told the servants to fill six stone vessels with **water**. After they were filled, Jesus instructed the servants to draw out some of the **water**. Meanwhile, but unknown to the servants, it had become **wine**.

When the **wine** was poured out, the Master of the wedding ceremony said the new **wine** tasted much better than the old **wine**. (John 2:1–11). i.e., the Old Covenant. This miracle, the first of Jesus' *'Sign Miracles'*, is linked to an undertaking by His Father which was recorded by His servant Isaiah.

> *"Ho! Everyone who thirsts, Come to the **waters**; and you who have no money, come, buy and eat. Yes, come, buy **wine** and milk without money and without price." "For as the heavens are higher than the earth* [as revealed in the Second Day], *so are My ways higher than your ways, and My thoughts than your thoughts."* (Isaiah 55:1 & 9).

When the **water** was turned into **wine**, it represented Jesus' blood. Again, water is the building block for every living cell. Wine and milk are God's blessings without price as promised in Isaiah (55:1). This miracle is also a vivid portrayal of how Jesus can change a person's life. When Jesus enters our lives we become a *'New Creation'* as earlier ways are forsaken and life's choices and desires become new. This happens through Jesus, God's chosen vessel, from whom when His side was pierced, **blood** and **water** flowed from Him. Red wine, which in spiritual terms is representative of the life-blood of Jesus, is explained physiologically in the book of Leviticus.

> *"For the life of the flesh is in the blood, and I have given it to you upon the altar to make atonement for your souls; for it is the blood that makes atonement for the soul."* (Leviticus 17:11). The word atonement means: *'To Cover'*.

In Jewish belief red wine is seen as being the blood of grapes. And red wine is what those who believe in Jesus partake of at the meal of Holy Communion as they remember His wounds and death on a borrowed cross on the outskirts of Jerusalem.

The Second Pillar of Wisdom is described in Proverbs 9:2.

'She has mixed her wine'.

The Second Pillar of Wisdom is PROPHETIC PERFECT in that it points to the life of Jesus that was in His blood and which has the power to cleanse and to divide us from our sin.

For those who may not be familiar with this mixing of wine (blood) by a factor of two, this will become much clearer when we come to consider the Sixth Day, the Sixth Appointed Time of the LORD (The Day of Atonement), and the Sixth Pillar of Wisdom. The sprinkling and mixing of two bloods is how the Day of Atonement was to be observed. And, says Paul, when Jesus the *'man'* died, at the same time Jesus the *'God Man'* in the imagery of His Father also died. In making such an assertion, what is its Scriptural justification?

When Paul was on his way to Jerusalem to celebrate the day of Pentecost and when he had reached the town of Miletus, Paul summoned the elders of the church in Ephesus to join him, and there he said to them:

> *"Therefore take heed to yourselves and to all the flock, among which the Holy Spirit has made you overseers, to shepherd the church of God which He purchased with His own blood."* (Acts 20:28).

What does Paul mean – that God has purchased us: **"...with His own blood."** In his second letter to the church in Corinth (5:19), Paul explains what he had said to the church elders:

"God was in Christ reconciling the world to Himself."

Reconcile means: *'To mend a broken relationship'*. This is how Jesus enables us to be joined to Him – as He is with His Father in a reciprocal Godly union. It is further evidenced in what Jesus said: *"I and My Father are one."* (John 10:30). When Jesus healed a paralyzed man at the Pool of Bethesda, those who were *'religious'* opposed Him. *'Therefore the Jews sought all the more to kill Him, because He not only broke the Sabbath, but also said that God was His Father, making Himself equal with God.'* (See John 5:1-23). It was because He made Himself equal with God which made them so angry.

To understand how the blood of Jesus is more effective than the blood that was mixed under the first Covenant, the Old Covenant (The Mosaic Covenant that God had made with His people Israel), the respected theologian, Dr. E. W. Kenyon, explains this in his booklet, THE BLOOD COVENANT.

> The blood of Jesus cleanses, instead of merely covering. The first covenant did not take away sin, it merely covered it. It did not give eternal life, or the new birth. It gave a promise of it. It did not give fellowship with God. It gave a type of it.

God's *'New Covenant'* with mankind, to grant forgiveness for sin that was made effective from the time when Jesus died on the cross – Jesus who is described in the Bible as being the Son of God and the Son of Man – His blood, His life, is then summarised in the words of the Second Pillar of Wisdom:

'She has mixed her wine'. (Proverbs 9:2).

> *For He* [God] *made Him* [Jesus] *who knew no sin to be sin for us, that we might become the righteousness of God in Him.'* (2 Corinthians 5:21).

OUR BLOOD AND HIS BLOOD

An additional life Merism is the way which human blood can cause pathological distress, can function with Jesus' blood which can result in new life and sanctification. This is why the taking of red wine at Holy Communion is so highly appropriate. Blood, of course, is essential, and there can be no life without it. Yet man is famously incapable of making his own blood as he is also incapable of saving himself.

Blood is made up of four elements: Plasma; Red Blood Cells; White Blood Cells; and Platelets. The most prolific is Plasma, and contributes to just over half of the human blood supply. Red Blood Cells come next and haematologists have affirmed that they constitute about 44 per cent of our blood supply. Their main function is to transport oxygen around the body.

Third are our White Blood Cells, and their main purpose is to fight infection. In volume they constitute less than one per cent of our blood supply.

Lastly are our Platelets. Again they form less than one per cent of the human blood supply. Our Platelets main purpose is to form blood clots when we cut or are injured, and so control and minimise the escape of blood from our blood vessels. Blood clotting can happen internally and externally.

For every individual – almost without exception – there will be times when we will experience health problems, such as a debilitating illness or some other malady. Blood tests are a primary method in determining the cause of an illness and if treated correctly, can result in bodily restoration. Because all can become innocent victims of numerous types of pathogens, which can also include certain types of blood disorders, confirms that the quality, quantity and purity of blood is of major importance.

In the way that temptation can be a never-ending spiritual battle, blood disorders which can affect our bodily lives can result in similar but physical challenges. However this is where the blood of Jesus can be so effectual, for because Jesus was pure and righteous, He is able by His blood to grant us cleansing and deliverance from our sin. In spiritual terms, if you have been *'Born Again'*, think of it as the time when you received a blood transfusion from Jesus.

The Hebrew Feast of Unleavened Bread demonstrates how the righteousness of Jesus can remove the unrighteousness of people – that which is not of the Father but is of this world. Therefore what is needed is the accepting of His righteousness to eradicate our unrighteousness. Thus as God on the Second Day divided the waters above the firmament from the waters below the firmament, so Jesus is able to separate and deliver us from our errant ways (that is providing we give Him our consent)

The Second Day, the Second Appointed Time of the LORD and the Second Pillar of Wisdom - **'She has mixed her wine'** – they contain spiritual insight for our enabling to see how the blood of Jesus is *'The Way, the Truth and the Life'* (John 14:6) that leads to godliness and contentment. This was confirmed by the apostle John when he wrote:

> *But if we walk in the light as He is in the light, we have fellowship with one another, and the blood of Jesus Christ God's Son cleanses* [it divides] *us from all sin.* (1 John 1:7).

****

THE THIRD DAY, THE THIRD APPOINTED TIME OF THE LORD, THE THIRD PILLAR OF WISDOM

Then God said, "Let the waters under the heavens be gathered together into one place, and let the dry land appear"; and it was so. And God called the dry land Earth, and the gathering together of the waters He called Seas. And God saw that it was good. Then God said. "Let the earth bring forth grass, the herb that yields seed, and the fruit tree that yields fruit according to its kind, whose seed is in itself, on the earth"; and it was so. And the earth brought forth grass, the herb that yields seed according to its kind, and the tree that yields fruit, whose seed is in itself according its kind. And God saw that it was good. So the evening and the morning were the third day.
(Genesis 1:9–13).

In his study of the Psalms, Eric Lane points out that grasses and plants often indicate human frailty. e.g., *'As for man, his days are like grass; as a flower of the field, so he flourishes.'* (Psalm 103:15). The Third Day was the day **before** the Sun and Moon appeared to establish the Earth's seasons. So how did plants produce seed and fruit if there were no seasons?

Following His death, as a gardener sows his seed, so the body of Jesus was placed in a garden tomb. (John 19:41–42). Three days later, an angel announced His resurrection to the two Marys – and: *'His countenance was like lightning and his clothing as white as snow.'* (Matthew 28:3). The angel then told them to go and tell His disciples that Jesus had risen.

In Hebrew the number three exemplifies *'Resurrection'*. This is why it follows that Jesus was meant to remain in the tomb for three days and nights before He arose from the dead.

Many, both then and today, view the resurrection of the dead as something which is impossible, or unattainable. However, in His discussion with Martha, Jesus informed her:

> "I am the resurrection and the life, He who believes in Me, though he may die, he shall live." (John 11:25).

Jesus, having said: "I am the resurrection", is it not assuring the grasses, herbs and fruit trees which bore seed and fruit; that they also appeared on a Third Day? (Genesis 1:11).

Later, Jesus informed His disciples:

> "I am the vine, you are the branches. He who abides in Me, and I in him, bears much fruit; for without Me you can do nothing." (John 15:5).

Jesus in announcing Himself as 'The Vine', was it not the fruit of the vine – as Jesus points out – which was uppermost in His thoughts, for it was the fruit of the vine, the grape, which featured so much in His teaching about the effectiveness of His Own blood? Jesus also said to His disciples:

> "Do you not say, 'There are still four months and then comes the harvest'? Behold, I say to you, lift up your eyes and look at the fields, for they are already white for harvest!" (John 4:35).

Here Jesus was not alluding to field plants, but to Jews and to Gentiles who would come to depend on Him. This included that at the end of His time of ministry, Jesus would die. Yet after three days and three nights – as the pattern is seen in the Third Day of Creation – Jesus would rise from the earth.

It was on the Third Day that the first grasses, herbs and trees appeared bearing seed and fruit whose seed was in the fruit.

This was repeated by the perfect timing of the resurrection of Jesus, which, most likely, took place at the timing of the Third Festival of the LORD, the Feast of Firstfruits. Firstfruits being described for the first time in Genesis 1:11–13.

Early in Israel's history, when the children of Israel were waiting to enter the Promised Land, God told Moses how he was to instruct the people to give thanks for what would be the first of their three seasonal harvests. The Barley Harvest.

Being a farmer's son, I witnessed the timing of a harvest may vary; depending on the type of seed, when it was sown, and the Sun and the Moon – the four seasons. This is why for the Feast of Firstfruits (unlike Passover and Unleavened Bread) no date is given; only the day. The Feast of Firstfruits was always to be held on a First Day of a week – the Day when the darkness of a tomb gave way to the resurrection of Jesus (the First Day being when the light overcame the darkness).

God's instruction for His people's observance of the Feast of Firstfruits is characterised by God's assurance of a harvest.

> *And the LORD spoke to Moses, saying, "Speak to the children of Israel, and say to them: 'When you come into the land which I give to you, and reap its harvest, then you shall bring a sheaf of the **firstfruits** of your harvest to the priest. He shall wave the sheaf before the LORD, to be accepted on your behalf; on the day **after** the Sabbath the priest shall wave it.'* [God's instruction is clear; the Feast of Firstfruits was always intended to take place on the First Day of a week]. *"And you shall offer on that day, when you wave the sheaf, a **male lamb** of the first year, without blemish, as a burnt offering to the LORD."* (Leviticus 23:9–12).

From the above there is zero any doubt. On whichever day of the week the barley harvest commenced (and it would not have been on a Sabbath) the offering of a *'male lamb without blemish'* – a male lamb without fault – and the giving of thanks to God, was *not* to take place until the First Day of the week after the next weekly Sabbath. Being grateful to God for His provision, the First Day of the week was the most appropriate day for Jesus to have risen from the dead. Thus for Paul in his belief that Jesus had risen, Paul confirmed his belief in recording the precise Day of Jesus' resurrection.

> *But now is Christ risen from the dead and has become the* ***firstfruits*** *of those who have fallen asleep.* (1 Corinthians 15:20). Notice Paul's recalling of the Feast of Firstfruits.

In a meeting with Scribes and Pharisees, Jesus said *"Three Days and Three Nights"* had been set-aside from when He would die and be buried, to when He would rise from death.

> *"For as Jonah was* ***three days*** *and* ***three nights*** *in the belly of the great fish, so will the Son of Man be* ***three days*** *and* ***three nights*** *in the heart of the earth."* (Matthew 12:40).

It was on the Third Day that God gathered the seas, next the dry land. It was the same period of days and nights (three), the same elements (the seas and the dry land), and the same sequence as Jonah was in the sea, followed by when Jesus was buried (as a seed is buried) in the earth (the dry land).

In his commentary on the book of Genesis, GLEANINGS IN GENESIS, Arthur Walkington Pink (1886–1952), writes:

> In the third day's work our Lord's resurrection is typically set forth. Thus it is in our type. Beyond doubt, that which is foreshadowed on the third day's work is resurrection. It is in the record concerning this third day's work that we read: *"Let the dry land appear."* (Verse 9). Previously, the earth had been submerged, buried beneath the waters.

But now the land is raised above the level of the seas; there is resurrection, the earth appears. But this is not all. In verse 11 [Genesis 1:11] we read, *"And let the earth bring forth grass"*, etc. Hitherto death had reigned. No life appeared upon the surface of the desolate earth. But on the third day the earth is commanded to: *"Bring Forth."*

Not on the second, not on the fourth, but on the third day was life seen upon the barren earth! Perfect is the type for all who have eyes to see. Wonderfully pregnant are the words, *"Let the earth bring forth"* to all who have ears to hear. It was on the third day our Lord rose again from the dead *'according to the Scriptures'*. According to what Scriptures?

Do we not have in these 9th and 11th verses of Genesis 1, the first of these Scriptures, the primitive picture of our Lord's resurrection?

When A. W. Pink – in the mid-twentieth century he was one of the most respected expositors of the Christian faith – wrote of the conjunction of the Third Day of Creation to the resurrection of Jesus, his conviction must have caused many to rethink their previous hypothesis about the Third Day.

Luke records it was three days after Jesus had died – *and not until He was sat at a **table** with two of his disciples in the village of Emmaus* – that Jesus made Himself known to them.

> *Now it came to pass, as He sat at the **table** with them, that He took bread, blessed and broke it, and gave it to them. Then their eyes were opened and they knew Him; and He vanished from their sight. And they said to one another, "Did not our heart burn within us while He talked with us on the road, and while He opened the Scriptures to us?"* (Luke 24:30–32). Note: The table was already in situ.

Later, and during the same evening, Jesus appeared again, this time to eleven of His disciples in Jerusalem. As with the first time, it was at a table that was already in situ.

> *Later He appeared to the eleven as they sat at the **table**; and He rebuked their unbelief and hardness of heart, because they did not believe those who had seen Him after He had risen.* (Mark 16:14).

Jesus then showed them the nail marks in His hands and feet. The Hebrew word for *'Friend'* means: TWO HANDS. Wisdom and its Third Pillar provides the reason for the Third Day:

> **'She has also furnished her table.'** (Proverbs 9:2).

Wisdom in naming a table as its Third Pillar is befitting, for it identifies Jesus' resurrection with the two harvest meals He shared with His disciples at the two tables.

A table – the most important item in a home where people can be gathered together – was referred to by David when he wrote Psalm 23, of how Jesus was to frustrate His enemies. *'You prepare a **table** before me in the presence of my enemies.'* (Psalm 23:5). Note especially Matthew 27:62–66.

In Malachi 1:7–13, we read of certain priests who profaned the LORD's name and sneered at His table and His provision. They said: *"The table of the LORD is defiled; and its fruit, its food, is contemptible."* (verse 12). They neither respected the LORD's table, or what the wine and the bread represented.

When His disciples were arguing as to who was the greatest among them, Jesus said the greatest was the one who served others, and that if they were prepared to do so, they would be able to sit, eat and drink at *"My table in My kingdom"* as His honoured wedding guests. (Luke 22:24–30).

For some after such a cruel act of pain and suffering, the resurrection of Jesus after three days and three nights may be difficult to accept. Perhaps as hard as it is to accept that plants and trees could produce seed and fruit on the Third Day before the Sun and the Moon appeared the following day, the Fourth Day, to prepare the Earth for its seasons?

The apostle Paul was aware of this acute difficulty, and so he addressed this issue about Jesus rising from the dead in his first letter to the Church in the city of Corinth. Paul stated why he believed Jesus had risen from the dead. In fact Paul staked his life on the fact that Jesus had risen.

> *Now if Christ is preached that He has been raised from the dead, how do some among you say that there is no resurrection from the dead? But if there is no resurrection of the dead, then Christ is not risen. And if Christ is not risen, then our preaching is empty and your faith is also empty. Yes, and we are found false witnesses of God, because we have testified of God that He raised up Christ, whom He did not raise up – if in fact the dead do not rise. For if the dead do not rise, then Christ is not risen. And if Christ is not risen, your faith is futile; you are still in your sins!* (1 Corinthians 15:12–17).

Paul knew for certain that Jesus had risen from the dead for he had spoken to Him on the road to Damascus. (Acts 9:3-4). Many years later, after his arrest in Jerusalem, Paul was able to witness to the Roman commander of how he came to faith by describing his face-to-face encounter with Jesus.

> "...*suddenly a great light from heaven shone around me.*" (Acts 22:6).

When Paul was blinded by a *'Great Light* (recalling the light of the First Day of the week and of Jesus who is the *'Light of the world*) and hearing Jesus saying to him: *"...why are you persecuting Me?"* (Acts 9:1-4), His appearance and His words were sufficient to convince Paul that the dead can indeed be raised to life a second time.

Continuing in his first letter to the Church in Corinth, Paul adds to what he has said by describing his own expectation of rising from death, and then linking this to the resurrection of Jesus. (Note: I quoted verse twenty on page 78).

> *If in this life only we have hope in Christ, we are of all men the most pitiable. But now Christ is risen from the dead, and has become the **firstfruits** of those who have fallen asleep. For since by man* [the first Adam] *came death, by Man* [the second Adam, the *'Son of Man'*, Jesus] *also came the resurrection of the dead.* (1 Corinthians 15:19-21).

Regarding the Christian faith and triumphing over death, the writer of Hebrews has a simple yet straightforward way of describing what faith is. *'Now faith is the substance of things hoped for, the evidence of things not seen.'* (Hebrews 11:1).

The unknown writer then refers to a number of earlier saints as examples of many who had been faithful to God and what they had experienced. Having recalled some of God's true and faithful servants, the writer goes on to say:

> *Women received their dead raised to life again. Others were tortured, not accepting deliverance, that they might obtain a better resurrection. Still others had trial of mockings and scourgings, yes, and of chains and imprisonment. They were stoned, they were sawn in two, were tempted, were slain with the sword. They wandered about in sheepskins and goatskins, being destitute, afflicted, tormented – of whom the world was not worthy.* (Hebrews 11:35-38a).

Of these *'Of whom the world was not worthy'*, it was because they had overcome any fear of death by their faith. Of these ordinary people – but truthfully extraordinary – they knew that suffering is not the end. Jesus had earlier said about life:

"Most assuredly, I say to you, unless a grain of wheat falls into the ground and dies, it remains alone; but if it dies, it produces much grain." (John 12:24). i.e., Resurrection Life.

The willingness of sufferers to die for Jesus, and yet still live, is a reminder of how God addressed the children of Israel concerning His promise of granting them victory over death.

"I will ransom them from the power of the grave; I will redeem them from death. O Death, I will be your plagues! O Grave [Sheol] I will be your destruction!" (Hosea 13:14).

Having been redeemed to know *'FREEDOM'*, believers will be able to join Jesus at His Wedding table. Wisdom has set-aside the places at His table. We do not have to do a thing but say **"YES"** to Wisdom's invitation by having invited the Master Craftsman into our lives.

THREE EQUATES TO 'DIVINE COMPLETENESS'

1. On the Third Day grasses that yielded seed and trees which bore fruit appeared. (Genesis 1:12–13).

2. The Third Appointed Time of the LORD is the Hebrew Harvest Festival of Firstfruits. (Leviticus 23:9–14).

3. After three days and nights of being buried in the earth, Jesus rose from the dead. (Mathew 12:40).

4. The Third Pillar of Wisdom – *'She has also furnished her table'* (Proverbs 9:2b). This is the Lord's table.

To complete the Third Day, I now turn to Mark's account of the resurrection of Jesus. Notice again the *'Large Stone'*. This *'Large Stone'* and its proximity to Jesus, is similar to the *'Large Stone'* Joshua set in place next to the Ark of the Covenant – God's Dwelling Place. (See pages 17–18).

> *Now when the Sabbath was past, Mary Magdalene, Mary the mother of James, and Salome bought spices, that they might come and anoint Him. Very early in the morning, on the first day of the week, they came to the tomb when the sun had risen. And they said among themselves, "Who will roll away the stone from the door of the tomb for us?" But when they looked up, they saw that the stone had been rolled away – **for it was very large**. And entering the tomb, they saw a young man clothed in a long white robe sitting on the right side; and they were alarmed. But he said to them, "Do not be alarmed. You seek Jesus of Nazareth, who was crucified. He is risen! He is not here. See the place where they laid Him. But go, tell His disciples – and Peter – that He is going before you into Galilee; there you will see Him as He said to you."* (Mark 16:1–7).

Jesus, who has *'Rolled Away'* the reproach of our wrongdoing, it means we can be clothed with His robes of righteousness.

A CLOSING THOUGHT

Earlier I pointed out the parallel of the three days and nights when Jonah was in the darkness of the great sea creature, and the three days and nights when Jesus was in the darkness of the tomb. There is a further link. Jonah said: *"Weeds were wrapped around my head."* (Jonah 2:5). For Jesus, weeds weaved into a crown of thorns (John 19:2), a Corona, were wrapped around His head by Roman soldiers when preparing Him for crucifixion. God, however, rescued them both – and both after three days and three nights.

THE FOURTH DAY, THE FOURTH APPOINTED TIME OF THE LORD, THE FOURTH PILLAR OF WISDOM

Then God said, "Let there be lights in the firmament of the heavens to divide the day from the night; and let them be for signs and seasons, and for days and years; and let them be for lights in the firmament of the heavens to give light on the earth"; and it was so. Then God made two great lights: the greater light to rule the day, and the lesser light to rule the night. He made the stars also. God set them in the firmament of the heavens to give light on the earth, and to rule over the day and over the night, and to divide the light from the darkness. And God saw that it was good. So the evening and the morning were the fourth day. (Genesis 1:14–19).

It is the Sun which radiates its light and its heat unfailingly, the Moon that reflects the Sun's light, and the tilt of the Earth from its vertical axis by twenty three degrees, by which God has given to the Earth's inhabitants their four seasons. And by observing the timing of the four seasons, we know when to sow our seed and when to gather our crops. If for any reason this order was to change – even by just a little – it would impact on our harvests and our ability to survive.

Concerning the Kingdom of God, Jesus spoke of it as:

"The kingdom of God is as if a man should scatter seed on the ground, and should sleep by night and rise by day, and the seed should sprout and grow, he himself does not know how. For the earth yields crops by itself: first the blade, then the head, after that the full grain in the head."

*"But when the grain ripens, immediately he puts in the sickle, because the **harvest** has come."* (Mark 4:26-29).

Here Jesus refers to night and day and His Kingdom as being like a harvest field. For the harvest and sickle Jesus referred to, sometime later (after Jesus had died and rose from the dead) His disciple John – who was in exile on the island of Patmos as a punishment for preaching that *"Jesus is Lord"* – was told to record the details of a vision he had received.

The vision John had received was as follows.

Then I heard a voice from heaven saying to me, "Write; Blessed are the dead who die in the Lord from now on." "Yes," says the Spirit, "that they may rest from their labors, and their works follow them." Then I looked, and behold, a white cloud, and on the cloud sat One like the Son of Man, having on His head a golden crown [a Corona] *and in His hand a sharp sickle. And another angel came out of the temple, crying with a loud voice to Him who sat on the cloud, "Thrust in Your sickle and reap, for the time has come for You to reap, for the **harvest** of the earth is ripe." So He who sat on the cloud thrust in His sickle on the earth, and the earth was reaped.* (Revelation 14:13-16).

Once again, God's Kingdom is likened to a harvest field. The Earth's harvests can only take place as a result of the Earth and the Moon's circumnavigation of the Sun; the Sun and the Moon not being featured until the Fourth Day. The Fourth Appointed Time of the LORD, the Feast of Weeks (Exodus 34:22), is when Jewish people celebrate their Wheat Harvest.

It was also at this Appointed Time that Jesus gifted the Holy Spirit to His disciples, for them to become His servants, His reapers, in the fields of the world that He, together with His Father and the Holy Spirit, had created. (See Hebrews 1:2).

Earlier, Jesus had also said to His disciples:

"The harvest truly is plentiful, but the laborers are few. Therefore pray the Lord of the harvest to send out laborers into His harvest." (Matthew 9:37-38).

The Hebrew celebration of the Feast of Weeks takes place seven weeks and one day (fifty days) after the people have celebrated the Feast of Firstfruits. In Hebrew this Feast is known as *'Shavuot'*. In Greek it is known as *'Pentecost'*.

When the disciples were filled with the Holy Spirit on the Day of Pentecost – Feast of Weeks – about one-hundred-and-twenty disciples were in the city of Jerusalem. (Acts 1:15). When Solomon dedicated the first Temple in Jerusalem, one-hundred-and-twenty priests sounded their trumpets and praised the LORD, saying: *"For He is good, for His mercy endures forever."* It was then *'...that the house, the house of the LORD, was filled with a cloud.'* (See 2 Chronicles 5:11-14).

This Cloud, indicating the *'Sovereignty of God'* which filled the House of God in Jerusalem in the days of King Solomon, was not unlike the *'Sovereignty of God'* which filled the place where the disciples were gathered – and in the same city, Jerusalem. Likewise this Cloud may have been of similar appearance to the *'White Cloud'* that John observed in his Revelation on the island of Patmos. (Revelation 14:14-16)

Included in his address to a large crowd of Jewish people on the Day of Pentecost – at least three thousand – Peter quoted what Joel had written about what he and the other disciples had just experienced. Joel's name means: *'The LORD is God'*.

But this is what was spoken by the prophet Joel: "And it shall come to pass in the last days, says God, that I will pour out My Spirit on all flesh..." (Acts 2:16-17a).

Peter continued by referring to what God had promised Joel.

"I will show wonders in heaven above and signs in the earth beneath: Blood and fire and vapor of smoke. The sun shall be turned into darkness and the moon into blood, before the coming of the great and awesome day of the LORD. And it shall come to pass that whoever calls on the name of the LORD shall be saved." (Acts 2:19-21). See Joel 2:28-32.

Is it not assuring how Peter chose these words from Joel for his message to his fellow Jews on the Day of Pentecost? When Peter said God would turn the Sun into darkness – as first happened when Jesus was dying and confirmed when God turned His face from His Son because of the imposition of our sin upon His Son: *"My God, My God, why have your forsaken Me?"* (Mathew 27:46) – and the Moon (a full Moon) would be turned into blood – as first took place when Jesus' face was covered by His blood – earlier God had said to Joel:

"The threshing floors shall be full of wheat and the vats shall overflow with new wine and oil." (Joel 2:24).

God's assurance links Israel's wheat harvest – the Feast of Weeks – to the Sun and the Moon, for which, according to Genesis 1:14, one of their purposes was for them to act as *'Signs'*. These *'Signs'* include the eight long-term influences which the Sun and Moon have upon the Earth. In Hebrew, eight is the number for *'Superabundant Fertility'*. Therefore, after the great flood that flooded the earth, in Genesis 8:22, we read of what God said about these eight Merisms.

"While the earth remains,
Seedtime and harvest,   (1st & 2nd signs)
Cold and heat,   (3rd & 4th signs)
Winter and summer,   (5th & 6th signs)
And day and night, shall not cease."   (7th & 8th signs)

In addition to God's declaration, when Isaiah wrote about the children of Israel's sinfulness (see Isaiah 30) and how in pursuing their own ways with little or no regard to their relationship with God, God reminded them of His grace and His mercy. God reminded them that while the earth remains, it is He who sends the rain to water their seed in the ground (Isaiah 30:23), for their animals to feed in large pastures, and for there to be rivers and streams of living water. (verse 25).

'Moreover...' – as God indicated, there is to be another day –

> ...*the light of the moon will be as the light of the sun, and the light of the sun will be **sevenfold**, as the light of seven days, in the day that the* LORD *binds up the bruise of His people and heals the stroke of their wound.* (Isaiah 30:26).

Within this sevenfold prophecy there seems to be a specific reason for the increase in intensity in the Moon and the Sun's appearance. But what does this sevenfold prophecy mean?

Perhaps the nearest mosaic – an adjective that adds meaning to Moses' name – concerns three Hebrew slaves, Shadrach, Meshach and Abednego. Their names mean: *'God is gracious', 'Who is like God?',* and *'God has helped'*. i.e., *'The LORD is gracious in binding up the bruises and healing the wounds of His people'*. For disobeying Nebuchadnezzar's blasphemous edict, the three slaves were told they would be thrown into a burning fiery furnace that was to be heated to **sevenfold** its normal temperature. Once the furnace was so hot that those who stood near its entrance were struck down, the three Hebrew slaves were bound before being cast into the flames. For Nebuchadnezzar, what he saw was not what he had expected. As Nebuchadnezzar gazed into the flames he saw not three men, but four, and he said of the fourth: *"...the form of the fourth is like the Son of God."* (Daniel 3:25). The Fourth has been shown to Jews and Gentiles as *'The Son of God'*.

Again via Isaiah, when God's prophet prophesied about the Jewish people being restored to their own land – which in truth is God's land – (and also the Gentiles being included in my Master's Sevenfold Plan), Isaiah wrote:

> *Arise shine; for your light has come! And the glory of the LORD is risen upon you. For behold, the darkness shall cover the earth, and deep darkness the people; but the LORD will arise over you, and His glory will be seen upon you, the Gentiles shall come to your light, and kings to the brightness of your rising.* (Isaiah 60:1–3).

This brightness applies not to the Sun, but to God's Son. (N.B., the Sun's rising is due to the Earth turning on its axis which gives the appearance of the Sun rising, not the other way round). Though the Sun and the Moon are inferior, they are nevertheless associated with God's glory and the glory of His Son. In this same chapter in Isaiah, the LORD declares:

> *"The sun shall no longer be your light by day, nor for brightness shall the moon give light to you; but the LORD will be to you an everlasting light, and your God your glory."*

> *"Your sun shall no longer go down, nor shall your moon withdraw itself; for the LORD will be your everlasting light, and the days of your mourning shall be ended. Also your people shall all be righteous; they shall inherit the land forever, the branch of My planting the work of My hands, that I may be glorified."* (Isaiah 60:19–21).

Clearly there are other aspects of the Sun, the Moon and the Earth for which this is not the time or the place to expand. However there is one aspect that is clearly apparent: Our lives are wholly dependent on them. Similarly, without God's Plan in providing both Jews and Gentiles with the gift of His Son, it would be impossible for us to be reconciled to God.

Following His resurrection, Jesus said to His disciples:

"Go into all the world and preach the gospel to every creature. He who believes and is baptized will be saved; but he who does not believe will be condemned." (Mark 16:15–16).

However Jesus told them to wait until they had received the Holy Spirit. Jesus said to them:

"Behold, I send the Promise of My Father upon you; but tarry in the city of Jerusalem until you are endued with power from on high." (Luke 24:49).

Having waited until the time of the Feast of Weeks, in Peter's message to his fellow Jews to repent and be baptised, Peter's plea was in full accordance with the Fourth Pillar of Wisdom.

She has sent out her maidens, she cries out from the highest places of the city, "Whoever is simple, let him turn in here!" (Proverbs 9:3–4a).

Is this city Jerusalem? It certainly appears so, for Wisdom's Messenger (The Holy Spirit) links Jerusalem to the heavenly city that is Zion. Jerusalem is the earth-bound city where:

1. It was here that God chose to place His name: *"Yet I have chosen Jerusalem that My name may be there..."* (2 Chronicles 6:6). Jerusalem belongs to God.

2. Jesus' disciples, who were Jews, were filled with the Holy Spirit on the Day of Pentecost (Feast of Weeks).

3. And after Peter had preached the Gospel to Jews only, approximately 3,000 Jews came to faith in Jesus and acknowledged Him as their Messiah. (Acts 2:41).

In Hebrew the gender for *'Wisdom'* the *'Holy Spirit'* and for those who will attend Jesus' marriage supper, is Female. For the Male counterpart, Scripture confirms the fact that:

> *"For your Maker is your husband, the LORD of hosts is His name; and your Redeemer is the Holy One of Israel; He is called the God of the whole earth."* (Isaiah 54:5).

Before we turn to the Fifth Day and the other invited guests, the Gentiles, it is important to remember why the Jewish people were chosen first. Jesus said to His disciples:

> *"Do not go into the way of the Gentiles, and do not enter a city of the Samaritans. But go rather to the **lost sheep** of the house of Israel. And as you go, preach, saying, 'The kingdom of heaven is at hand.'"* (Matthew 10:5-7).

Why did Jesus tell His disciples to preach the *'GOOD NEWS'* of the Gospel to Jewish people, but not to the Gentiles?

During His time of ministry, Jesus was once approached by a lady from Canaan who pleaded with Him to show mercy to her demon-possessed daughter. At first Jesus refused to speak to her! Only when His disciples had said to Him: *"Send her away..."*, for they saw her as an interloper, did Jesus finally speak to the lady. He explained to her: *"I was not sent except to the **lost sheep** of the house of Israel."* Yet although the lady worshipped and pleaded with Him on behalf of her distressed daughter, Jesus still refused to expel the demon.

Jesus said to her: *"It is not good to take the children's bread and throw it to the little dogs."* Not until she reminded Him that even little dogs were entitled to a few crumbs that fell from the Master's table – in doing so, she wisely referred to His resurrection! – did Jesus finally respond to her request. Why? Because she had *'Great Faith'*. (Matthew 15:21-28).

My question is: *"If Jesus was so focussed on reaching out to people, why was He not willing at first to consider the plight of this non-Jewish lady?"* Might it have been because of the fallen state of the Jewish people, that so many had, according to Jeremiah, strayed so far from God that they were blind and deaf to what God had once meant to them? In the following passage from Jeremiah, it is God who is speaking.

> *"My people have been **lost sheep**. Their shepherds have led them astray; they have turned them away on the mountains. They have gone from mountain to hill; they have forgotten their resting place."* (Jeremiah 50:6).

And in a similar manner, God also spoke through Ezekiel.

> *For thus says the Lord God: "Indeed I Myself will search for My **sheep** and seek them out. As a shepherd seeks out his flock on the day he is among his scattered **sheep**, so will I seek out My **sheep** and deliver them from all the places where they were scattered on a cloudy and dark day."* (Ezekiel 34:11–12).

In Paul's letter to the believers in Rome, Paul addresses this issue of the Gospel being preached first to the **'Lost Sheep'** of the house of Israel, then afterwards to the Gentile nations.

> *"I am not ashamed of the Gospel of Christ, for it is the power of God to salvation for everyone who believes, for the Jew **first** and also the Greek"* [Gentiles]. (Romans 1:16).

Following Paul's close-encounter with Jesus one of his most important meetings was held in a synagogue in Antioch and some of the Jews who were present, believed. (Acts 13:14–49). However some of the Gentiles who were also present pleaded with Paul to explain to them at his next meeting on the next Sabbath, Paul's *'GOOD NEWS'* about Jesus.

A week later, when many in Antioch assembled to hear what Paul had to say, some of the Jews who were in attendance became envious, and turned against him, accusing Paul of blasphemy! As a result, Paul said to them:

> *"It was necessary that the word of God should be spoken to you **first** [Jews being the Fourth Pillar of Wisdom]; but since you reject it, and judge yourselves unworthy of everlasting life, behold we turn to the Gentiles."* (Verse 46).

The conclusion of Paul's statement was that the timing for the Gentiles was rapidly approaching and was in accordance with the Fifth Pillar of Wisdom. This, of course, was what Jesus had originally intended for Paul when He appeared to him on the road to Damascus; for as He said to Ananias before he went to lay his hands on Paul (Saul) for his sight to be restored, Jesus said to him:

> *"Go, for he is a chosen vessel of Mine to bear My name before the Gentiles, kings, and the children of Israel."* (Acts 9:15).

However, did Paul ever waver in believing his fellow Jews would come to faith in Jesus? Having stated the Gospel was to be preached **first** to the Jewish people (Romans 1:16), further on Paul says that God will never abandon them. His question and then his answer: *"I say then, has God cast away His people? Certainly not!"* (Romans 11:1).

In Romans chapters 9, 10, and 11, Paul states though at the time only a minority of Jewish people had received Jesus as their Saviour, nevertheless, a day would come when Jewish people would be grafted back into the cultivated olive tree. The olive tree is often seen as a Biblical metaphor for the Kingdom of God. Gentiles should never assume that Jewish people have been rejected by God in favour of themselves.

Paul continued with his teaching on this vital subject by explaining his insight into the destiny of the Jewish people.

> *For I do not desire, brethren, that you should be ignorant of this mystery, lest you should be wise in your own opinion, that blindness in part has happened to Israel* [the Jewish people] *until the fullness of the Gentiles has come in. And so all Israel will be saved, as it is written: "The Deliverer will come out of Zion, and He will turn away ungodliness from Jacob; for this is My covenant with them, when I take away their sins."* (Romans 11:25–27). See Isaiah 59:20 & 27:9.

Paul was quoting two prophesies from Isaiah. If Paul had chosen to he could easily have included a promise God made with His servant Hosea. To begin with however, God told Hosea to marry Gomer, a prostitute, as a lesson of how God's people had turned away from God by committing harlotry. The following is what God instructed Hosea to do.

> *The word of the LORD that came to Hosea the son of Beeri, in the days of Uzziah, Jotham, Ahaz, and Hezekiah, kings of Judah, and in the days of Jeroboam the son of Joash, king of Israel. When the LORD began to speak by Hosea, the LORD said to Hosea: "Go, take yourself a wife of harlotry and the children of harlotry, for the land has committed great harlotry by departing from the LORD". So he went and took Gomer the daughter of Diblaim, and she conceived and bore him a son.* (Hosea 1:1–3).

God, who has always honoured His undertaking to bless the Jewish people as a result of His promise to Abraham that his descendants would be as the *'Stars of the Heaven'* (Genesis 22:17), He continued by saying to them through Hosea:

> *"**I will** betroth you to Me forever; yes, **I will** betroth you to Me in righteousness and justice, in loving-kindness and*

*mercy; **I will** betroth you to Me in faithfulness, and you shall know the LORD."* (Hosea 2:19–20).

Notice God's *'Sevenfold Triple-Lock'* to the children of Israel when He says: *"I will"*. Despite their unfaithfulness, God has not changed His mind about Abraham's many descendants.

In Deuteronomy there is a written guarantee that God will never turn His back on the Jewish people. The following is what God has declared concerning His ancient people Israel.

"For you are a holy people to the LORD your God; the LORD your God has chosen you to be a people for Himself, a special treasure above all the peoples on the face of the earth. The LORD did not set His love on you nor choose you because you were more in number than any other people, for you were the least of all peoples; but because the LORD loves you, and because He would keep the oath which He swore to your fathers, the LORD has brought you out with a mighty hand, and redeemed you from the house of bondage, from the hand of Pharaoh king of Egypt. Therefore know that the LORD your God, He is God, the faithful God who keeps covenant and mercy for a thousand generations with those who love Him and keep His commandments."
(Deuteronomy 7:6–9).

It is because God is a trustworthy keeper of His promises and always shows mercy to those who love Him and keep His commandments, that God has never given-up on the Jewish people, despite the fact that only a small minority of them have remained faithful to Him throughout their history.

Therefore as a result of God's Covenant with Abraham, it means that God's Covenant people are the abiding essence of the Fourth Day, the Fourth Appointed Time of the LORD – The Feast of Weeks – and the Fourth Pillar of Wisdom.

By way of a reminder, the Fourth Pillar of Wisdom states:

'She has sent out her maidens, she cries out from the highest places of the city [Jerusalem?], *"Whoever is simple, let him turn in here!"* (Proverbs 9:3-4a).

It is sad that the word *'Simple'* is often used as a pejorative term. But this is not what was intended in the Fourth Pillar of Wisdom. A more meaningful term would be *'Without Guile'*. An example of this is in what Jesus said of Nathanael:

"*Behold, an Israelite indeed, in whom is no guile* [deceit]." (John 1:47).

THE SUN AND THE MOON – PRIMARY CLOCKS

Not until the Fourth Day, the most accurate measurement of time is the way Atomic Clocks measure time by monitoring the resonant frequency of atoms. Atomic Clocks are known as *'Primary Clocks'*. When growing up on my father's farm, I was often impressed in that he knew when it was lunch-time, not by looking at his watch, but by observing the reliable positioning of the Sun in the sky. The events that took place on the Fourth Day are the genesis of the Primary Clock.

To bring to a close the Fourth Day, the Fourth festival, the Feast of Weeks, and the Fourth Pillar of Wisdom, I conclude with what Peter Sammons has said about times and seasons.

To follow God's pattern for life in the annual calendar, as set out in Leviticus 23, we need to use the same calendar, the Lunar Calendar. In this each month begins when the new moon appears in the night sky, and each day begins at nightfall. *'He* [God] *appointed the moon for seasons; the sun knows its going down.'* (Psalm 104:19). So that all the Biblical Feasts happen on days set by the Lunar Calendar, is the Biblical calendar still important to God, or has it been replaced in some way?

Since the Biblical Feasts mark out the *'High Points'* of God's redemptive purposes, and also express God's view of the history of mankind, it is superfluous to ask if His calendar and His Appointed Festivals are still important. Rather, we should be asking: *"How do they speak to us today?"* The Lord Jesus died on the *'Feast of Passover'* and was raised from the dead on the *'Feast of First Fruits'*.

We can say with certainty that Jesus fulfilled the prophetic meaning of these Feasts, and on the actual days that they occurred.

Peter Sammons' conviction (which is in accordance with my own conviction) is that the Hebrew/Lunar Calendar – the Biblical Calendar – is inclusive of two reliable events.

1. It speaks of the birth, life, death, resurrection, and the completed mission of the Master Craftsman Himself. The Lord Jesus.

2. It speaks of how Jesus became a Saviour to the Jewish people (the Jewish people being the Fourth Pillar of Wisdom), then just a few months later to the Gentiles (the Gentiles being the Fifth Pillar of Wisdom).

These events as outlined firstly in Genesis – events which have been made known to every individual who has the ability to discern what the heavens declare – lead on to the Fifth Day, the Fifth Appointed Time of the LORD, and the Fifth Pillar of Wisdom.

****

THE FIFTH DAY, THE FIFTH APPOINTED TIME OF THE LORD, THE FIFTH PILLAR OF WISDOM

Then God said: "Let the waters abound with an abundance of living creatures, and let birds fly above the earth across the face of the firmament of the heavens." So God created great sea creatures and every living thing that moves, with which the waters abounded, according to their kind, and every winged bird according to its kind. And God saw that it was good. And God blessed them, saying: "Be fruitful and multiply, and fill the waters in the seas, and let birds multiply on the earth." So the evening and the morning were the fifth day. (Genesis 1:20–23).

The Fifth Appointed Time of the LORD, the Feast of Trumpets, takes place in the Lunar Calendar on the first day of the seventh month. Then the LORD spoke to Moses saying:

*"Speak to the children of Israel, saying: 'In the seventh month, on the first day of the month, you shall have a sabbath-rest, a memorial of blowing of trumpets, a holy convocation. You shall do no customary work on it; and you shall offer an offering made by **fire** to the Lord.'"* (Leviticus 23:23–25). See also Numbers 10:1–10.

In Hebrew the number five equals *'Grace'*, – *'Being justified freely by His grace through the redemption that is in Christ Jesus.'* (Romans 3:24). Jewish tradition subscribes to God's Plan that the first Feast of Trumpets took place at the time Abraham took Isaac his son to Mount Moriah (the same location where God's Son would be crucified). Abraham then took the wood he had placed on his son's back – as a wooden cross would be placed on the back of God's Son – to prepare an altar of *fire* on which he would obey God by offering up his son. On the Third Day, after Abraham arrived at Moriah – the Third Day speaks of resurrection – as Abraham took a knife to slay his son – as a Roman soldier took his spear and plunged it into the side of Jesus – the Angel of the LORD called to Abraham and told him not to slay Isaac. It was then that...

> *...Abraham lifted his eyes and looked, and there behind him was a ram* [male] *caught in a thicket* [thorns] *by its horns. So Abraham went and took the ram and offered it up for a burnt offering instead of his son. And Abraham called the name of the place, The-Lord-Will-Provide;* [in Hebrew: יהוה יְרָאֶה! Adonai Yireh] *as it is said to this day, "In the Mount of the LORD it shall be provided."* (Genesis 22:13-14).

God's command on the Fifth Day to the sea creatures to fill the seas, then for birds to fill the air and earth by multiplying – God's allocation for marine and avian life – is mirrored in a command that Jesus gave to His disciples.

> *"Go therefore and make disciples of all the nations* [the land based inhabitants], *baptizing them* [plunging them into water as the marine creatures] *in the name of the Father and of the Son and of the Holy Spirit."* (Matthew 28:19).

On the occasion of the Feast of Weeks (the Fourth Feast), the disciples were baptised in the Holy Spirit and from Jerusalem they went out and preached the Gospel – but only to Jews. Later when resting on the roof of a house in Joppa (Joppa means *'Beauty'*), Peter had a vision and he also heard a voice. The inference of what Peter saw and heard was that it was now time for him, a Jew, to go to the Gentiles. The next day Peter travelled to Caesarea, in Samaria, to the home of the Centurion Cornelius, and explained the Gospel to Gentiles. While Peter was speaking, the Holy Spirit descended upon all who were listening. (Acts 10:1–48). What Peter and his six friends who had travelled with him saw and heard – *'For they heard them speak with tongues and magnify God'* (Acts 10:46) – mirrored the Fifth Day and the Fifth Jewish festival, the Feast of Trumpets. It was, as Jesus had said to His disciples: *"...you shall be witnesses to Me in Jerusalem, and in all Judea and Samaria, and to the end of the earth."* (Acts 1:8b).

The reason for God's Plan as declared in the last command Jesus gave to disciples, can be found in Revelation 14:6-7.

> *Then I saw another angel flying in the midst of* **heaven**, *having the everlasting gospel to preach to those who dwell on the* **earth** *– to every nation, tribe, tongue, and people – saying with a loud voice* [as with the sound of a trumpet], *"Fear God and give glory to Him, for the hour of His judgment has come; and worship Him who made* **heaven** *and* **earth**, *the* **sea** *and springs of water."*

Note the harmony with the Fifth Day: The heavens, the earth, and the sea. (Genesis 1:20-23). The Fifth Pillar of Wisdom:

> **'As for him who lacks understanding...'** (Proverbs 9:4).

The Fifth Pillar of Wisdom indicates that a new list of guests, those who had little or no knowledge of God, that it was intended for them to be added to attend the Master Craftsman's marriage supper. Thus for Cornelius his family and friends, they were among the first Gentiles to be included to join with the first guests, Jewish people, to be baptised as believers and to be filled with the Holy Spirit.

Paul also knew it was within God's Plan for Gentiles to form, as with Jewish people, the chosen Bride of Christ.

> *Therefore remember that you, once Gentiles in the flesh...* [the Fifth Pillar of Wisdom] *...that at that time you were*

*without Christ, being aliens from the commonwealth of Israel and strangers from the covenants of promise, **having no hope and without God in the world**. But now in Christ Jesus you who once were far off have been brought near by the blood of Christ. For He Himself is our peace, who has made both one* [Jews and Gentiles], *and has broken down the middle wall of separation, having abolished in His flesh the enmity, that is the law of commandments contained in ordinances, so as to create in Himself one new man from the two, thus making peace, and that He might reconcile them both to God in one body through the cross, thereby putting to death the enmity.* (Ephesians 2:11-16).

The word *'Peace'* Paul includes in his letter to the Ephesians is the Hebrew word *'Shalom'*, and has a number of meanings, including *'Inner Wholeness'* and *'Harmony in God'*. Shalom is a word – it is also a deeply held concept – that is often used to enquire about a person's state of health and well-being.

In this letter to the Ephesians, Paul explains how Jews and Gentiles have become reconciled to God through the Cross. Paul then adds to this in his letter to the Galatians.

Then after fourteen years I went up again to Jerusalem, with Barnabas, and also took Titus with me. And I went up by revelation, and communicated to them that gospel which I preach among the Gentiles, but privately to those who were of reputation, lest by any means I might run, or had run, in vain.

Yet not even Titus who was with me, being a Greek, was compelled to be circumcised. And this occurred because of false brethren secretly brought in (who came in by stealth to spy out our liberty which we have in Christ Jesus, that they might bring us into bondage), to whom we did not yield submission even for an hour, that the truth of the gospel might continue with you. But from those who seemed to be something – whatever they were, it makes no difference to me; God shows personal favouritism to no man – for those who seemed to be something added nothing to me. But on the contrary, when they saw that the gospel for the uncircumcised [Gentiles] *had been committed to me, as the gospel for the circumcised* [Jews] *was to Peter (for He who worked effectively in Peter for the apostleship to the circumcised also worked effectively in me toward the Gentiles) and when James, Cephas and John, who seemed to be pillars* [of the Fourth Pillar], *perceived the grace that had been given to me, they gave me and Barnabas the right hand of fellowship, that we should go to the Gentiles and they to the circumcised* [Jews]." (Galatians 2:1–9).

In this letter Paul explains at length why it was necessary for an initial period of time to be set-aside for the Gospel to be preached to the Jews, then when the timing was right, for the Gospel to be preached to the Gentiles.

God's Plan – Day Five – to include Gentiles, is in line with the Fifth Pillar of Wisdom. For its intended outcome, Psalm 117 begins: *'PRAISE the Lord, all you Gentiles...'*

The Fourth Pillar of Wisdom symbolizes the Jewish people. **"Whoever is simple, let him turn in here!"** (Proverbs 9:4a).

The Fifth Pillar of Wisdom symbolizes the Gentiles. **"As for him who lacks understanding..."** (Proverbs 9:4b).

In my appraisal of the First Day, I referred to the assistance provided by Alan Stibbs from his book, HIS BLOOD WORKS. It is here I would like to quote again from what Stibbs has to say about Jews and Gentiles. In his opening remarks, Stibbs refers to Ephesians chapter two. (See pages 101 –102 where I have recorded the verses from Ephesians 2:11–16).

In the next four paragraphs, Stibbs assesses the relationship brought about by Jesus regarding the Jews and the Gentiles.

Verse thirteen [See Ephesians 2:13] comes in a paragraph that refers to the bringing in of [the] Gentiles, who had been complete outsiders, to become fellow citizens with the saints and full members of the family or household of God. [i.e., First the Jews. Second the Gentiles].

Hitherto, as the dividing wall of the Jewish Temple courts symbolized, they [being the Gentiles] had been both shut out from the nearer access to God and separated from full fellowship with Israel.

Now they are reconciled both to God and to man; and, says Paul in the same context, Christ abolished the enmity *'in His flesh'*, or through His incarnation and earthly life; and He actually achieved the full victory and slew the enmity by means of the cross.

It is, therefore, *'through the Cross'* that He reconciles them both unto God. When, therefore, Paul said previously that those once afar off are made nigh *'by the blood of Christ'*, he unquestionably means, as he immediately explains, that they [meaning Gentiles] are made nigh as a consequence of Christ's death upon the Cross.

During his early years as a disciple of Jesus, the apostle John was unlikely to have been aware of those attendees who would be present at Jesus' marriage supper. When it came to the time for the details to be made known to John, a voice came from the throne-room of God, saying to John:

> *Then he said to me, "Write: 'Blessed are those who are called to the marriage supper of the Lamb!'" And He said to me, "These are the true sayings of God." (Revelation 19:9).*

For those who have drawn near to God by the work of the Holy Spirit – including Gentiles as well as Jews – when Isaiah was considering the Gentile's future heritage, he prophesied:

> *And in that day there shall be a Root of Jesse, who shall stand as a banner to the people; for the Gentiles shall seek Him, and His resting place shall be glorious.'* (Isaiah 11:10).

Later, again from Isaiah, Isaiah wrote (See Isaiah 42:1 & 6b):

> *"Behold! My Servant whom I uphold, My Elect One in whom My soul delights! I have put My Spirit upon Him; He will bring forth justice to the Gentiles... As a light to the Gentiles, to open blind eyes." 'My Elect One'* is, of course, Jesus.

The above quotation is taken from the first of Isaiah's four Servant Songs. In Isaiah's Second Song – Isaiah 49:1-7 – the LORD Himself goes a step further by describing not only His own commitment to bring Jacob (Israel) back to Himself, but to explain how His Son will be *'As a light to the Gentiles...'*. The emphasis in Isaiah's Second Song is that God's grace is not to be restricted to just Israel, but that God will extend His grace and His mercy to every tribe and nation.

> *"And now the LORD says, who formed Me from the womb to be His Servant* [The Lord Jesus] *to bring Jacob back to Him, so that Israel is gathered to Him (For I shall be glorious in the eyes of the LORD, and My God shall be My strength). Indeed He says, 'It is too small a thing that You should be My Servant to raise up the tribes of Jacob, and to restore the preserved ones of Israel;* **I will also give You as a light to the Gentiles, that You should be My salvation to the ends of the earth.**' " (Isaiah 49:5-6).

Though Isaiah's four Servant Songs are featured among the many prophesies concerning Jesus which can be found in the

Old Testament Scriptures, it is sad that many Jewish people still do not read them in this context. Indeed, Jewish people have been consistently told by their religious leaders that Isaiah's four Servant Songs are related to themselves (Israel), and not to Jesus their Messiah. Yet the Fourth Pillar of Wisdom indicates that Jesus *is* their Messiah (the Christ) who first appealed to the Jewish people, then to the Gentiles – the Gentiles being the Fifth Pillar of Wisdom:

"As for him who lacks understanding..."

Isaiah's numerous prophecies and the Fifth Pillar of Wisdom – the Gentiles – are also referred to by David, the author of Psalm 22 (which is clearly Messianic and which I refer to a number of times in this study).

> 'All the ends of the world shall remember and turn to the LORD, and all the families of the nations shall worship before You.' (Psalm 22:27).

Having considered the first Five Days, the Sixth Day comes next. So far God's Plan has included the first Five Steps.

(1) Day One: How God's light overcame the darkness.

(2) Day Two: How righteousness justifies and leads to life, whereas sin is oppressive and leads to death.

(3) Day Three: How the emergence of plants and trees portrayed the emergence of Jesus from the grave.

(4) Day Four: How God's deep love of the Jewish people was that they might be the first to hear the Gospel.

(5) Day Five: How the Gentiles are included in God's Plan as beneficiaries of His grace and His mercy.

God's methodology within Creation (rather than theology for according the Desi Maxwell there is no word in Hebrew for theology), brings us to the incarnation of the *'One'* who was tasked with implementing my Master's Sevenfold Plan: the Master Craftsman Himself. C. G. Bartholomew and R. P. O'Dowd, who I quoted earlier, have something important to say in their chapter *'Jesus, the Wisdom of God'* and their conclusion about Wisdom. Readers may find their thoughts about Biblical/Spiritual Wisdom as a helpful beginning to the introduction to the Sixth Day, the Sixth Appointed Time of the LORD, and the Sixth Pillar of Wisdom.

> The Incarnation [the birth of Jesus] signals a dramatic shift in the storyline of the Bible. Wisdom in the Old Testament focuses on the created order, what can be called God's structure for the world. But it does not give attention to the overarching direction of the creation – how the world will move from creation to fall and back to a redeemed new creation again.
>
> Wisdom in the New Testament affirms the creation order of the Old Testament, but it focuses it historically in the mystery of God's purposes bound up in Jesus, the Agent who saves creation and leads it to the destiny God always intended for it. In Christ, God Himself has taken on the human role of redemption and blessing previously assigned to Israel, and then given it back not just to Israel, but also to all the nations and peoples of the world.
>
> Wisdom then embodies the new, radical way for us to live in God's world and play our role in proclaiming and conforming to His kingship.

According to Bartholomew and O'Dowd's assessment, both Creation and Redemption are included in God's Plan (and are described in the Bible's first volume: The book of Genesis).

Having gifted the food and wine for His marriage supper – thus having prepared *'The Lord's Table'* – Jesus then invites the first guests who are from among the Jewish people.

> **She has sent out her maidens, she cries out from the highest places of the city** [Jerusalem], **"Whoever is simple, let him turn in here!"**

Then having sent out a similar invitation to the Gentiles...

> *"As for him who lacks understanding"*

...what further confirmation is needed other than what the LORD Himself promised Isaiah?

> *"Also the sons of the foreigner* [Gentiles] *who join themselves to the LORD, to serve Him, and to love the name of the LORD, to be His servants – everyone who keeps from defiling the Sabbath, and holds fast My covenant – even them I will bring to My holy mountain, and make them joyful in My house of prayer."* (Isaiah 56:6-7a).

When writing to the new believers in Rome – Gentiles – Paul was overawed in recognising how God's Plan now included Gentiles as well as the Jewish people. The following is how Paul summarised the grace and mercy of God in extending His love to the two people groups who God had now reached out to set His seal upon by baptising them in the Holy Spirit.

> *Oh, the depth of the riches both of the wisdom and knowledge of God! How unsearchable are His judgments and His ways past finding out!* (Romans 11:33).

****

THE SIXTH DAY, THE SIXTH APPOINTED TIME OF THE LORD, THE SIXTH PILLAR OF WISDOM

Then God said, "Let the earth bring forth the living creature according to its kind: cattle and creeping thing and beast of the earth, each according to its kind"; and it was so. And God made the beast of the earth according to its kind, cattle according to its kind, and everything that creeps on the earth according to its kind. And God saw that it was good.

Then God said, "Let Us make man in Our image, according to Our likeness; let them have dominion over the fish of the sea, over the birds of the air, and over the cattle, over all the earth and over every creeping thing that creeps on the earth."

So God created man in His own image; in the image of God He created him; male and female He created them. Then God blessed them, and God said to them, "Be fruitful and multiply; fill the earth and subdue it; have dominion over the fish of the sea, over the birds of the air, and over every living thing that moves on the earth."

And God said, "See, I have given you every herb that yields seed which is on the face of all the earth, and every tree whose fruit yields seed; to you it shall be for food. Also, to every beast of the earth, to every bird of the air, and to everything that creeps on the earth, in which there is life, I have given every green herb for food"; and it was so.

Then God saw everything that He had made, and indeed it was very good. So the evening and the morning were the sixth day. (Genesis 1:24–31).

The Sixth Day is my Master Craftsman's pièce de-résistance, the coming together of His land-based creatures. But notice the personal pronouns used in Genesis one, verse twenty six.

> "Let <u>Us</u> make man in <u>Our</u> image, according to <u>Our</u> likeness." (Genesis 1:26).

The Hebrew name for God that appears in the first account of Creation is a plural noun. Man's Creator was: (1) The Father. (2) The Son. (3) The Holy Spirit. It was together that they created man. The Hebrew name in Genesis 1:1–2:3, 'ELOHIM', is the name that refers to the Trinity.

In what for many Bible scholars is seen as being the second account of Creation (Genesis 2:4–25), the Hebrew name that is used, 'LORD God', is a singular noun. The Hebrew name for LORD God is 'ADONAI'.

There are also other added features in the second account of Creation which do not appear in Creation's the first account. For example: the 'Tree of Life', the 'Tree of Knowledge of Good and Evil', the 'Fall of Man', and the 'Serpent'. And the Trinity is featured in the first account of Creation, but not in the second account. And also the naming of Adam and Eve does occur until Creation's second account.

The much respected theologian, John Metcalfe, in His book CREATION, and in his detailed analysis of the two opening chapters of the book of Genesis (the two accounts), explains.

> On opening the book of Genesis, perhaps the most remarkable feature to strike the reader is that there are two records of the Creation, not one. These differ immensely, not only in emphasis and direction but also in volume and form. The reason is spiritual, and no one can attain to the understanding of the Creation without that

spiritual knowledge. For the truth is that hidden in the records of Creation lies the revelation of Jesus Christ, quite apart from the record of Adam.

If Metcalfe's conclusion of the two accounts of Creation is that Jesus is featured in one of them – the first? – but is concealed, was His concealment intentional? If Metcalfe is correct, then it is quite feasible that a time would one day dawn when Jesus would visit the Earth in the image of His Father to solve the difficulty of man's separation from God.

But long before Jesus was born – and also since His birth – there has existed in mankind an awareness of who God is. This is recognised as *'Common Grace'* (as opposed to *'Saving Grace'*). Common Grace is the awareness in men and women of the dividing line between good and evil, for which we have a choice, and which has been endorsed upon our consciences not by evolution, but by God.

The apostle Paul wrote about Common Grace in his letter to the Church in Rome.

> *For when Gentiles, who do not have the law* [the Holy Scriptures], *by nature do the things in the law, these, although not having the law, are a law to themselves, who show the work of the law written in their hearts, their conscience also bearing witness, and between themselves their thoughts accusing or else excusing them.* (Romans 2:14–15).

On an occasion when Jesus spoke to a group of His fellow Jews, He explained to them God's Plan and how His life would come to an end. Luke recorded what Jesus said to them: *"And whoever does not bear his cross and come after Me cannot be My disciple."* Having spoken of crucifixion, He then explained what was involved in His Father's Plan.

"For which of you, intending to build a tower [or a house such as God's House], *does not sit down first to count the cost, whether he has enough to finish it – lest, after he has laid the foundation, and is not able to finish, all who see it begin to **mock** him, saying, 'This man began to build and was not able to finish.' "* (Luke 14:27-30).

Jesus having *'counted the cost in Gethsemane'*, arrested and put on trial, was **'mocked'** by those who passed judgement upon Him. Later as He was dying, they again **'mocked'** Him:

"He saved others; let Him save Himself if He is the Christ [meaning: *'The Messiah'*], *the chosen of God."* (Luke 23:35).

Saving Grace is what took place after Adam and Eve who had sinned, were clothed by God with tunics made from animal skins. But animal skins only gave a short-term covering for sin: never a long-term solution. The solution was prophesied by Micah when he wrote: *"But you Bethlehem Ephrathah, yet out of you shall come forth to Me the One to be Ruler in Israel."* (Micah 5:2). Many years later an angel of the LORD appeared to Joseph and informed him concerning Mary his fiancée:

"And she will bring forth a Son, and you shall call His name JESUS, for He will save His people from their sins." (Matthew 1:21).

In recalling Isaiah 49:1 (page 16), the birth of Jesus was in accordance with a PROPHETIC PERFECT PLAN.

*"Listen, O coastlands, to Me, and take heed, you peoples from afar! The LORD has called Me from the **womb**; from the matrix of My mother He has made mention of My name."*

In the way Israel's Tabernacle was designed for worship and the Holy-of-Holies was appointed as its innermost sanctuary, so, too, Mary's womb, her inner holiness, was appointed as a sanctuary for God's Son. At that time pregnancy scans were unknown of, but Joseph, who was called upon to act as a father in his *'Father's Place'*, was told both the gender and the name of Mary's child while God's Son was in embryo.

In this same Song (Isaiah 49), God's promise continues:

"And now the LORD says, who formed Me from the womb to be His Servant, to bring Jacob back to Him, so that Israel [the Jewish people and the Fourth Pillar of Wisdom] *is gathered to Him." "I will also give You as a light to the Gentiles* [the Fifth Pillar of Wisdom], *that You should be My salvation to the ends of the earth."* (Verses 5a & 6b).

Though Amos has been credited by some to have been only a minor prophet; nevertheless God informed His servant:

"Surely the Lord GOD does nothing, unless He reveals His secret to His servants the prophets." (Amos 3:7).

Based on this assurance, how the role of a prophet's ministry is to reveal God's future plans, in Psalm 2:7, it is recorded:

"You are My Son, today I have begotten You."

The Complete Jewish Bible renders God's declaration as:

"You are My Son, today I became Your Father."

In Hebrews 1:5 and 5:5, God's declaration is spoken of in the context that from the day of His birth, Jesus was appointed by His Father to function as our High Priest. Therefore this prophecy might prompt its reader to consider: *"Why did God appoint for the Sixth Day, the making of a Man in His Own image, rather than on one of His other five working days?"*

Additionally, *"Was God's decision about His Plans for His Son, including Mary's birth of His Son, so that the timing of His birth was intended to conform spiritually to the Sixth Day?"*

As man in God's image has been assumed to be linked to the Sixth Day, should we be asking: *"Is the Sixth Day linked to the Sixth Appointed Time of the* LORD, *the Day of Atonement* (in Hebrew *'Yom Kippur'*), *the day when the Hebrew prayer 'Avinu Malkeinu'* (meaning: *'Our Father, our King'*) *is prayed?"*

If God had a special purpose for the Sixth Day, which He saw as being *'Very Good'* – in a similar way as the Sixth Appointed Time is said to be a *'Holy Convocation'* (Leviticus 23:27) – was it because God had planned for there to be an intended link to join these two events? Viz., The making of a husband, next his wife on the Sixth Day; and the birth of Jesus, next His Church (its gender is female) on the Day of Atonement?

My suggestion is from the Day Jesus was born, Jesus was appointed to function as a High Priest and to attend to the role Aaron had played in the Tabernacle's Holy-of-Holies on the Day of Atonement. The Day of Atonement was the only day in the Lunar Year when the High Priest was allowed to enter the Holy-of-Holies. Is this why the Sixth Day and the Sixth Appointed Time – the Day of Atonement – that these two times are, to all intents and purposes, inseparable?

When the LORD spoke to Moses and laid down how his elder brother Aaron was to approach God in the Holy-of-Holies in the Tabernacle (remember the plans for the Tabernacle were laid down by God in Heaven), the LORD said to Moses:

> "Tell Aaron your brother not to come **at just any time** into the Holy Place inside the veil, before the mercy seat which is on the ark, lest he die; for I will appear in the cloud above the mercy seat." (Leviticus 16:2).

From God's instructions to Moses (passed on by Moses to his brother Aaron), it was essential for Aaron to obey God. Had he not done so, Aaron almost certainly would have died.

Why did God say that Aaron must keep strictly to His Plan for the Day of Atonement? Surely it was because this Day was always going to be a part of God's Plan for His Son (Saving Grace)? And so the foretelling of His birth, when Jesus was to enter this world in the form of a newly born child and as God's Son – announced first in Genesis 1:26 – is to be found in the Scriptures that Jesus so often referred to: in the writings of Moses, the Prophets and the Psalms.

In Margaret Barker's book, CHRISTMAS THE ORIGINAL STORY, Barker, former President of the Society for Old Testament Study, quotes Philo who saw the two accounts of Creation as being different. In his book ALLEGORICAL INTERPRETATION, Philo describes how he understood the book of Genesis.

Genesis 1:26, describes the Heavenly Adam, made in the image and after the likeness of God. Genesis 2:7 describes the man formed from dust. *"There are two types of men; the one a Heavenly Man* [Jesus], *the other an earthly man* [Adam]." (For clarity my emphasis has been added).

Barker refers to known spiritual principles to explain how the only day in the Hebrew calendar on which it would have been appropriate for Jesus to have been born, was on the LORD's Day of Atonement and in the Holy-of-Holies (first seen in the Tabernacle in the days of Moses, then the first and second Temples in Jerusalem). It has been said the Holy-of-Holies was at the epicentre of the world. i.e., *'Its navel'*.

Barker's conclusion is that although the Holy-of-Holies was the most appropriate location for the birth of Jesus to have taken place, nevertheless, as Barker continues to postulate...

...no place in the inn could well have been an allusion, there being no Logos in the Holy-of-Holies. The Firstborn and the Glory, the Logos, the pre-existent second person of the Trinity, was not born in the Holy-of-Holies and did not appear in His garments of Glory in Jerusalem. He was swaddled in a manger elsewhere. Barker's conclusion of His birthplace: *'The Expected in the Unexpected.'*

Following His birth, the swaddling material (I assume) Mary took with her to wrap her new-born Son in, may well have been similar to the white linen tunic Aaron was clothed with before entering the Holy-of-Holies on the Day of Atonement. Where Jesus was born and the events surrounding His birth, each of these special events was *'Pre-Planned'* by His Father.

In his letter to the Church in Philippi, Paul refers to Jesus as being revealed to man *'...in the form of God'.* Additionally that He was also born as a man.

> *Christ Jesus ... being in the form of God, did not consider it robbery to be equal with God, but made Himself of no reputation, taking the form of a bondservant, and coming in the likeness of men* [as seen by the shepherds soon after His birth]. *And being found in appearance as a man* [by the wise men who were guided from Jerusalem by a star], *He humbled Himself and became obedient to the point of death, even the death of the cross.* (Philippians 2:5b–8).

But does this mean that when Jesus was born He became less than God? No, of course not, *'For in Him dwells all the fullness of the Godhead bodily.'* (Colossians 2:9).

To assimilate these two signs (the Sixth Day and the Sixth Appointed Time – the Day of Atonement) is to note there is a third sign. The Sixth Pillar of Wisdom (PROPHETIC PERFECT) prompted the invitation Jesus shared with His disciples:

"Come, eat of my bread, and drink of the wine I have mixed." (Proverbs 9:5).

The Sixth Pillar of Wisdom's remit to mix wine (blood) is further explained in what Jesus said to His disciple Philip.

"He who has seen Me has seen the Father." (John 14:9).

Earlier Jesus had said: *"I and My Father are one."* [*Then the Jews took up stones again to stone Him.*] ((John 10:30-31).

"The wine I have mixed", recalls what God ordered Moses to say to Aaron when explaining how he was to observe the Day of Atonement. First a young bull was offered to God as a sin offering for Aaron and his family. Aaron then sprinkled some of the bull's blood on the Mercy Seat, the covering of the Ark of the Covenant which was located in the Holy-of-Holies.

Next a goat was sacrificed as a sin offering for the people, and some of its blood was also sprinkled on the Mercy Seat to mix with the blood of the young bull. This sprinkling and mixing of blood from two animals was done to show how the bull's blood that Aaron had presented as a token for himself as the High Priest, was to be mixed with the goat's blood that was a representative token for men and women. Dr. Stuart Sacks describes this sprinkling (and mixing) of blood as:

> The sprinkling of blood was to show that justice had been tempered by mercy.

Within God's Plan this act of the mixing of two bloods was carried out when Jesus was crucified. For the Centurion, who effectively was to repeat what Jesus had said earlier to His disciple Phillip, and had been tasked with confirming His death, after Jesus had died and in exercising his authority, said: *"Truly this Man was the Son of God!"* (Mark 15:39).

The Centurion's confession that he saw Jesus as: *"...this Man was the Son of God!"* – can be traced back forty weeks before Jesus was born to when Mary was informed by Gabriel:

> *"The Holy Spirit will come upon you, and the power of the Highest will overshadow you; therefore, also, that Holy One who is to be born will be called the Son of God."* (Luke 1:35).

THE FIRST ADAM AND THE LAST ADAM

When *'...the LORD God formed man of the dust of the ground'* (Genesis 2:7), He made it impossible for man to give birth. That being so, if man was ever to become a father – as God Himself is a Father – Adam needed an aide to whom he could be joined in marriage. To solve this difficulty, God made an opening in Adam's side and from the incision Adam's wife Eve was formed. (The Hebrew word for *'Side'* and *'Rib'* is the same – *'Tsela'* צלע). That which God did to Adam, a Roman soldier repeated when he made an incision in Jesus' side, and from His life-atoning blood His wife, the Church, was formed.

It was by a divine act God placed the first Adam in a *'Deep Sleep'* (Genesis 2:21) – *'An Induced Sleep'* – before He made an opening in his side to form his wife Eve. Next, Jesus, was placed in *'An Induced Asphyxiation'* by the cross (John 19:30) before a soldier was allowed to make an opening in His side to enable His Bride, His Church, to be formed.

Previous to this, before His side was pierced (Psalm 22:16 and Zechariah 12:10) and during His last Passover meal...

> *... Jesus took bread, gave thanks and broke it, and gave it to them, saying, "This is My body which is given for you." Likewise He also took the cup after supper, saying, "This cup is the new covenant in My blood which is shed for you."* (Luke 22:19-20).

When consuming wine during Holy Communion, though some absorption will occur in the mucous membrane, most takes place through the wall of the small intestine. The wine then permeates to unite with the person (eating the bread) and drinking the wine. The reason we do so is that *'...Christ may dwell in our hearts through faith'*. (Ephesians 3:17a).

The apostle Paul understood this spiritual meaning, and so he warned the Corinthian believers not to eat the bread and drink the wine without due respect and reverence. This is why Paul felt the need to caution his fellow believers.

> *Therefore whoever eats this bread or drinks this cup of the Lord in an unworthy manner will be guilty of the body and blood of the Lord. But let a man examine himself, and so let him eat of the bread and drink of the cup. For he who eats and drinks in an unworthy manner eats and drinks judgment to himself, not discerning the Lord's body.*
> (1 Corinthians 11:27–29).

At the time of His birth in Bethlehem, when Jesus made His debut as the *'Son of Man'* and the *'Son of God'*, was how Jesus entered this world via the veil between Heaven and Earth. At the end of His life, the Temple's veil was torn in two from above to below to confirm that the need for a veil to separate men and women from God was finally over.

It is because of these two events – the birth of Jesus and His death – that we can have true confidence in approaching the throne-room of God. The writer of Hebrews assures us:

> *For we do not have a high priest who cannot sympathize with our weaknesses, but was in all points tempted as we are, yet without sin. Let us therefore come boldly to the throne of grace, that we may obtain mercy and find grace to help in time of need.* (Hebrews 4:15–16).

Concerning John's declaration of Jesus as having been in the beginning with God (See John 1:1-5), Tom Wright asks:

> Many Jewish teachers had grappled with the age-old questions: *"How can the one true God be both different from the world and active within the world? How can He be remote, holy and detached, and also intimately present?"*

The answer to Tom Wright's two conundrums is explained in what Jesus went on to say to His disciple Philip.

> **"Do you not believe that I am in the Father, and the Father in Me? The words that I speak to you I do not speak on My own authority; but the Father who dwells in Me does the works."** (John 14:10)).

Partly in response to His disciples' confusion, Jesus added:

> *"I came forth from the Father and have come into the world. Again, I leave the world and go to the Father."* (John 16:28).

His words confirm that from when the *'Power of the Highest overshadowed'* Mary, Jesus was appointed to be made known to the world in the likeness of His Father. The reason was because Jesus had been destined by His Father to become our High Priest and for Him to enter this world through the veil which once divided Heaven from Earth. The long-term effect of putting God's Plan into action – the freeing up of our lives from sin and sin's condemnation – is, as Jesus taught:

> *"Therefore if the Son makes you free* [free from our sin], *you shall be free indeed."* (John 8:36).

When it comes to Jesus taking on the role of an intermediary between God and those He has created, there is a valid indication of this in a prophecy in the book of Isaiah.

This prophecy is then explained in the New Testament book of Hebrews, for which its principal message is that Jesus is our High Priest. (See Hebrews chapters one to ten).

> *There shall come forth a Rod from the stem of Jesse, and a Branch shall grow out of his roots.*
>
> *His delight is in the fear of the LORD, and He shall not judge by the sight of His eyes, nor decide by the hearing of His ears; but with righteousness He shall judge the poor, and decide with equity for the meek of the earth; He shall strike the earth with the rod of His mouth, and with the breath of His lips He shall slay the wicked. Righteousness shall be the belt of His loins, and faithfulness the belt of His waist.* (Isaiah 11:1 and 3–5).

What is included by Isaiah partly applied to Aaron who had been tasked with caring for the spiritual needs of his people, then to Jesus in saving the contrite and the penitent. Also included was the special clothing Aaron wore as he served God (Leviticus 16:4), and His one-piece linen garment Jesus had been wearing and was stripped of when He was being prepared for crucifixion. (John 19:23–24). When Jesus was crucified He was naked – *'Not Ashamed'* (Genesis 2:25) – that is without sin, like Adam had been naked before he sinned.

In Israel's community the role of the High Priest was crucial for his responsibility was to act as the people's intermediary before God. In doing so he performed a range of duties so that the nation might live as God's chosen people. Included in Aaron's role as High Priest, was one that was of much greater importance than all his other tasks. On the Day of Atonement (on the tenth day of the seventh month), the High Priest would not have worn his regular priestly robes. Instead, like Jesus, he would have clothed himself in a one-piece linen garment before entering the Holy-of-Holies.

Aaron's role was transitional. A time would come when God would send His Son and men and women would no longer be reliant on an individual who was restricted by his humanity.

> *But Christ [Messiah] came as High Priest of the good things to come, with the greater and more perfect tabernacle not made with hands, that is, not of this creation. Not with the blood of goats and calves, but with His own blood He entered the Most Holy Place once for all, having obtained eternal redemption.* (Hebrews 9:11-12).

The recalling of goats and calves and of Jesus *'Entering the Most Holy Place'*, likens His entrance (His birth) to when the High Priest would have entered the Holy-of-Holies on the Day of Atonement. In John's Revelation we read:

> *Then the temple of God was opened in heaven, and the ark of His covenant was seen in His temple.* (Revelation 11:19).

This *'Ark of His Covenant'* refers to God's dwelling place. Of comparable appointment was the Ark of the Covenant made by Bezalel (whose name means: 'IN THE SHADOW OF GOD'). (Exodus 35:30-35). During King David's reign, the Ark of the Covenant (In Hebrew, *'Ark'* is masculine) went missing. Eventually and in Ephrathah (Bethlehem), it was said: *'We found it in the fields of the woods.'* (Psalm 132:6-8).

About one thousand years later – *'With the Lord one day is as a thousand years and a thousand years is as one day'* (2 Peter 3:8) – when shepherds from the *'Fields of Bethlehem'* found Jesus dwelling in a manger (Luke 2:8-16), the manger's role took over the role to the Ark of the Covenant. This included the possibility that the two – the manger and Israel's Ark of the Covenant – could have been made of the same material, Acacia wood, and have been of similar size and appearance. Length: 43 ¾". Width: 26 ¼". Height: 26 ¼ ". (Exodus 37:1).

THE METHODOLOGY OF MIDRASH

In about the year 2000, my wife and I were invited to attend a conference in Manchester, England, arranged to encourage believers to further add to their understanding the Biblical and Hebrew aspects of their Christian faith.

David Davis, from the Mount Carmel fellowship in Israel, was one of the guest speakers. Encouraged by his lectures, we purchased a copy of David's book THE ELIJAH LEGACY and soon began to discover the hidden meaning of what is known in Scripture as *'The Methodology of Midrash'.*

In his book, David writes at length about the origins and the purpose of Midrash. David explains.

> There is an ancient Jewish concept of understanding prophecy which is called *'Midrash'.* The word comes from a root that means: *'To Search'.* Hebrew commentators and writers understood and applied four basic modes of interpretation to Scriptural prophecy.

David then provides a brief summary of the four modes of discovery behind the Hebrew understanding of Midrash.

> SIMPLE – Plain, literal sense of the text.
>
> HINT – A word, phrase, or other element in the text which hints at things of which the writer was not aware, and which is not conveyed by the *'Simple'* meaning.
>
> SEARCH – An allegorical application of the text.
>
> SECRET – A hidden meaning.

In his explanation of the term *'Midrash'*, David continues:

Midrash is a Hebrew methodology [way] of understanding prophecy. Prophecy is not only a specific or *'Simple'* prediction, but also contains *'Hints'* and a *'Search'* for deeper meaning. Sometimes there can be a *'Secret'* meaning. Therefore there are often multiple fulfilments, or layers, of a single prophecy.

In John Allen-Piper's book, CREATION UNLIMITED, its author also writes about the *'Secret Meaning'* of prophecy.

The most important example of this level of Scripture surrounds the *'Aleph'* and the *'Tav'*, the first and last letters of the Hebrew alphabet, equivalent to the *'Alpha'* and *'Omega'* in the Greek. These two letters occur as the central letter in the seven-word menorah verse of Genesis 1:1. This word is untranslatable, but nevertheless occurs extensively throughout the Old Testament including seven times in Genesis 1 that describes God's work of Creation.

In Rabbinic literature it is often referred to as the *"Word of Creation"*. John's Gospel identifies Jesus as the *'Word of Creation'* [as explained in John 1:1-3]. Here John becomes the second witness of David's declaration in Psalm 33:6. *"By the word of the LORD the heavens were made; and all the host of them by the breath of His mouth."* The properties of the first verse of Genesis are central to God's claim to be the Creator.

A further hint of the Methodology of Midrash can be viewed in Leviticus 16:29-34 where an instruction is given for what was to take place on the Day of Atonement. This passage explains how for Aaron, who had been chosen by God and then anointed to be set-aside as High Priest to minister in the Tabernacle, that it was in the Tabernacle's Holy-of-Holies that he was to make an atonement for God's people: *"...in his father's place ... and put on holy garments."* (Leviticus 16:32).

In this chapter, nothing is said about Aaron's father as being of any connected relevance. In fact, although Aaron's father was Amram, a Levite who was married to his father's sister Jochebed, this is about all we know of Aaron's father – apart, that is, in the meaning of their three names.

Names in the Bible can carry hidden meanings – such as with the three Hebrew slaves (page 89). This is why in Hebrew there exists what is known as *'The Theology of Names'*. Biblical names can carry concealed truths, and may at times be featured to point to God's historic and future plans. Briefly, the meaning of their three names is as follows.

AARON – means *'High Mountain'*.

AMRAM – means *'Exalted'*.

JOCHEBED – means *'Yahweh is Glory'*.

One day Jesus took along with Him three of His disciples, Peter, James and John, to a High Mountain (Aaron) where He was transfigured – Exalted (Amram) – before them as His face shone like the Sun and His clothes became as white as the light surpassing the whiteness of the garments worn by Aaron on the Day of Atonement. The three disciples were then highly honoured to witness a revelation of Yahweh's Glory (Jochebed). Peter said to Jesus: *"Lord, it is good for us to be here."* While Peter was still speaking to Jesus, *'...a bright cloud overshadowed them'* and a voice came out of the cloud as if from heaven saying to His three disciples:

"This is My beloved Son in whom I am well pleased. Hear Him!" (Mathew 17:1–5).

When the instruction for Aaron to serve *'...in his father's place'* was given, it is doubtful that his father was still alive.

Aaron was eighty three years old when he and his younger brother Moses had left Egypt. (Numbers 33:38-39).

So who is this *'Father'* figure who is referred to in Leviticus 16:32? Could this be an allusion to the *'One True God'*, of whom Jesus said: ***"He is My Father"***, who enabled Jesus to be formed in Mary's womb, then to be made known first to the Jewish people (Acts 3:26), the Fourth Pillar of Wisdom, and next to the Gentiles (Acts 11:18), the Fifth Pillar of Wisdom?

The Day of Atonement (See Leviticus 16:1-34) focussed on the time when Jesus would emerge on His Father's behalf in order to serve others; He who was born thirty years before His public service commenced when He was placed in a manger to become the focus of His Father's Sevenfold Plan.

Matthew's genealogy of Jesus records He was not born of Israel's priestly tribe, the tribe of Levi, from whom Aaron was a direct descendent, but that He was of the tribe of Judah and of David's line, David who reigned as a King. The book of Hebrews explains why the priesthood needed to be changed – as the Law of Moses needed to be changed – to inaugurate a Holy, righteous and revised priesthood. The three verses which follow are taken from Hebrews chapter seven.

> *For the priesthood being changed, of necessity there is also a change of the law. For He of whom these things are spoken* [meaning Jesus] *belongs to another tribe, from which no man has officiated at the altar. For it is evident that our Lord arose from Judah, of which tribe Moses spoke nothing concerning priesthood.* (Hebrews 7:12-14).

THE FIFTIETH YEAR OF JUBILEE

There is a further detail about the Day of Atonement which could have a direct link with the birth of Jesus. It is an order promulgated by His Father about the fiftieth year of Jubilee. In Leviticus it states that in the year of Jubilee, the Day of Atonement was to be kept as a time of consecration and to be celebrated with the blowing of trumpets. At the fiftieth year, the Day of Atonement was a *'Day'* of great rejoicing.

Regarding three of the LORD's festivals, God said to Moses:

"Three times you shall keep a feast to Me in the year." (Exodus 23:14). This was later expanded when God added: *"Three times in the year all your men shall appear before the Lord, the LORD God of Israel."* (Exodus 34:23).

For the men of Israel, God's instruction was that they were to make three annual pilgrimages to Jerusalem. These times – they are known as *'Pilgrim Festivals'* – are the times when the Jewish people give thanks for their three annual harvests.

The first harvest (Barley) is celebrated in the spring at the time of Firstfruits. The second harvest (Wheat) is celebrated at the time of the Feast of Weeks – fifty days after Firstfruits. The third harvest (Fruits, Nuts and Berries) is celebrated at the time of the Feast of Tabernacles; the Hebrew festival which takes place at the close of the agricultural year.

So why do Jewish people not ascend to Jerusalem on the Day of Atonement? Why is this a time of holiness, self-denial and fasting? And what is it about the fiftieth year of Jubilee that makes this *'Day'* a day of much rejoicing? It is because in the year of Jubilee, the Day of Atonement was the time appointed for the men (accompanied by their wives and children) to return to their ancestral towns and villages from where they were born and grew up – and *not* to go up to Jerusalem.

Known as the *'Year of Jubilee'*, it is a Sabbath year that is to be held in the year following a period of seven times of seven years (forty nine years of planting and harvesting) and is to be kept as a celebratory occasion. i.e., A year of Good News. God's instruction for the fiftieth year of Jubilee is as follows.

And the LORD spoke to Moses on Mount Sinai, saying, "Speak to the children of Israel, and say to them: 'When you come into the land which I give you, then the land shall keep a sabbath to the LORD. Six years you shall sow your field, and six years you shall prune your vineyard, and gather its fruit; but in the seventh year there shall be a sabbath of solemn rest for the land, a sabbath to the LORD. You shall neither sow your field nor prune your vineyard." (Leviticus 25:1-4).

In verses 5-7 of Leviticus 25, the LORD tells Moses what the people of Israel were to do in keeping each seventh year as a year of rest. i.e., They were Sabbath Years. Having covered His Introduction, the LORD's instruction continues:

*"And you shall count seven sabbaths of years for yourself, seven times seven years; and the time of the seven sabbaths of years shall be to you forty-nine years. Then you shall cause the trumpet of the Jubilee to sound on the tenth day of the seventh month; on the **Day of Atonement** you shall make the trumpet to sound throughout all your land. And you shall consecrate the fiftieth year, and proclaim **liberty** throughout all the land to all its inhabitants. It shall be a Jubilee for you; and each of you* [i.e., This applies to the menfolk] *shall return to his possession, **and each of you shall return to his family**."* (Leviticus 25:8-10).

When the Day of Atonement occurred in a fiftieth year of Jubilee, it had a much greater impact on Jewish society than it had at other times. The first reason was spiritual, then physical, for it was on *this* Day of Atonement that God had said it was to be a *'Day'* that was to be observed as a day of **"Liberty"**. For the men folk of Israel, it meant they were to return to their ancestral towns and villages – the place of their birth lineage. i.e., Their ancestors. (Leviticus 25:10).

With prophetic foresight did God's instruction apply to what Luke wrote of how for Joseph, *'...because he was of the house and lineage of David'* (Luke 2:1-7), that with his betrothed wife Mary, Joseph had **no choice** but to go up to Bethlehem? Fittingly it was in Bethlehem (Ephrathah) – *'Bet Lehem'*, the *'House of Bread'* – the place where Joseph's forebears had originated, that Mary was to give birth to God's Son. And it was in Bethlehem an *'Ark'* for His dwelling, a lowly manger, was already in situ for the birth of God's Son. The phrase *'In Situ'* quintessentially is taken from the Latin: *'In Position'*.

Previously I said how Hebrew names can convey important messages, or meanings, such as the name Jesus. In Hebrew, *'Jesus/Yeshua'* means: *'Saviour'*. The same is true of numbers. For those wanting to learn how numbers – such as *'Seven'* and *'Fifty'* – connect with Scripture, Ethelbert W. Bullinger * has provided in his work of Biblical research, NUMBER IN SCRIPTURE, a comprehensive listing in Hebrew and Biblical watchfulness, the importance of numbers.

Concerning the number fifty, Bullinger explains its numerical positional meaning, and also its religious meaning.

Fifty is the number of Jubilee or deliverance. It is the issue of 7 x 7 (7^2), and points to deliverance and rest following a period of perfect consummation of time [such as 40 weeks].

---

* Born in Canterbury, Ethelbert W. Bullinger (1837 – 1913) was a descendent of the Protestant church reformer Johann Bullinger, who succeeded Zwingli, founder of the reformed church in Zurich in 1531. Bullinger was educated at King's College, London, and went on to become a distinguished scholar of languages.

Consummation, a term associated with marriage – marriage the time when a man and a woman come together for the first time as one flesh – one of the results of a marriage union is that when a child is conceived, then in the fullness of time, forty weeks, is the time for the mother to give birth. And after the child is born, when the mother's birth pains have ended, then for the mother rest is the byword. Perfect and fit for purpose for the birth of Jesus is not only the Day of Atonement, but also the fiftieth year of Jubilee.

For Mary, a virgin yet to be married, to be expecting a child could have led to family disgrace. However her vindication was that on receiving the news from the angel Gabriel about conceiving in her womb a Son who Mary was to name Jesus, Mary then made a covenant with Gabriel. This is similar as marriage is a covenant for two to become one to enable them to produce godly offspring. (Malachi 2:14–15).

When Mary was told that her expected Son would be known as the *"Son of God"*, Mary then declared a vow with Gabriel.

"Let it be to me according to your word." (Luke 1:38).

As a young woman, Mary's vow meant that if her father may have berated her for becoming pregnant outside of marriage, then her *'Shalom'* was the restraining order which God had placed upon her father. From a legal aspect, the following injunction is void of ambiguity, yet in essence it appears to have been intended **specifically** for Mary's protection.

> *"If a woman makes a **vow** to the LORD, and binds herself by some agreement while in her father's house in her **youth**, and her father hears her vow and the agreement by which she has bound herself, and her father holds his peace, then all her vows shall stand, and every agreement with which she has bound herself shall stand."* (Numbers 30:3–4).

THE BRIDEGROOM'S MARRIAGE SUPPER

For those who by their faith and trust will be attending Jesus' marriage supper, those who have made themselves ready by having replied *"YES"* to His invitation, the Sixth Pillar of Wisdom's application is to be seen in the body of God's Son.

> *"Come, eat of my bread, and drink of the wine I have mixed."* (Proverbs 9:5).

God's gift of salvation, His unstinting love, can be seen in what was made known to the apostle John.

> *Then one of the elders answered, saying to me, "Who are these arrayed in white robes, and where did they come from?" And I said to him, "Sir, you know." So he said to me, "These are the ones who come out of the great tribulation, and washed their robes and made them white in the blood of the Lamb. Therefore they are before the throne of God, and serve Him day and night in His temple. And He who sits on the throne will dwell among them. They shall neither hunger any more* [Bread/Manna. Exodus 16:10–36] *nor thirst anymore* [Wine. Luke 22:17–18)]; *the sun shall not strike them, nor any heat; for the Lamb who is in the midst of the throne* [the Lord Jesus] *will shepherd them and lead them to living fountains of waters. And God will wipe away every tear from their eyes."* (Revelation 7:13–17).

The mention in this Scripture of living waters is one we will come to when we come to and consider the Seventh Day. Meanwhile, and in bringing the Sixth Day to a close, I would like to include a section from what is essentially *'The Lord's Prayer for all believers'*. In knowing that the time was near for His task on Earth to be completed, Jesus gave thanks to His Father for enabling Him to accomplish all that He had set out to do. Jesus then prayed for His disciples.

However, there were numerous others – including those alive today – who Jesus wanted to include in His prayer. And so Jesus prayed:

> *"I do not pray for these alone, but also for those who will believe in Me through their word; that they all may be one, as You, Father, are in Me, and I in You; that they also may be one in Us, that the world may believe that You sent Me."* (John 17:20–21).

What is true of Jesus (and is true for us all), is that when His body was being formed in Mary's womb, His blood remained isolated from Mary's blood. And so when Jesus included in His prayer: *"...as You, Father, are in Me, and I in You..."*, His prayer recalled His Father was the source of His Holiness, for He received His righteousness, not from His mother Mary, but from His Heavenly Father. Mary's role in the birth of Jesus was to donate her womb as a sanctuary for Jesus. Mary had offered: *"Behold the maidservant of the Lord! Let it be to me according to your word."* (Luke 1:38). Thus as St. Paul wrote: *"The first man Adam became a living being." 'The last Adam became a life-giving spirit.'* (1 Corinthians 15:45).

Jesus' prayer came towards the end of His final Passover meal when He and His disciples recalled how the children of Israel had been set-free from slavery in Egypt. Passover then progressed to become Holy Communion, when we take of His bread and His wine – His body and His blood – to remind us of why Jesus came and why He died. This is why Holy Communion is so poignant, as we take of what we read in Proverbs concerning the Sixth Pillar of Wisdom:

> *"Come, eat of my bread, and drink of the wine I have mixed."*

****

THE SEVENTH DAY, THE SEVENTH APPOINTED TIME OF THE LORD, THE SEVENTH PILLAR OF WISDOM

Thus the heavens and the earth, and all the host of them, were finished. And on the seventh day God ended His work which He had done, and He rested on the seventh day from all His work which He had done. Then God blessed the seventh day and sanctified it [He made it Holy], *because in it He rested from all His work which God had created and made.* (Genesis 2:1-3).

Today with the help of physicians, life can sometimes be extended – I mean beyond seventy years. (Psalm 90:10). A hundred years is no longer unusual as more people live to an age a few years ago would have been sparse. However one aspect of living longer is that one third of our mortal lives can be taken up with sleeping. For those considered average, sleep can last for more than twenty-five years!

The reason we sleep is to rest – for we have been designed to do so. Any lack of rest and we can easily become morose; or maybe suffer from maladies that may affect our health? So why do we spend a third of our lives sleeping? And why is it that rest and the Seventh Day, a Day symbolic of rest, feature constantly in our physical and mental symmetry?

The Seventh Hebrew festival, the Feast of Tabernacles – in Hebrew *'Succot', "...the Feast of Ingathering at the end of the year, when you have gathered in the fruit of your labors from the field"* (Exodus 23:16) – mirrors the Seventh Day.

> *Then God blessed the seventh day ... because in it He rested from all His work which God had created...* (Genesis2:3).

The Feast of Tabernacles, the Seventh Appointed Time of the LORD, marks the time when Jewish people give thanks and rest: as in a very similar way God conducted Himself as He observed the Seventh Day by setting it aside for His resting.

THE FEAST OF TABERNACLES – OR THE FEAST OF BOOTHS

The Feast of Tabernacles, known also as The Feast of Booths, is the time when Jewish people make temporary shelters to dwell in during the seven days of this festival. These booths are a reminder of the temporary shelters that the children of Israel lived in during the forty years they journeyed through the wilderness – before God enabled them to enter and to dwell in the Promised Land.

The Promised Land – which geographically is at the centre of the world (its navel) – is where God once led Abraham to and where he and his family also dwelt in temporary shelters.

> *By faith Abraham obeyed when he was called to go out to the place which he would receive as an inheritance. And he went out, not knowing where he was going. By faith he dwelt in the land of promise as in a foreign country, dwelling in tents with Isaac and Jacob, the heirs with him of the same promise; for he waited for the city which has foundations, whose builder and maker is God.* (Hebrews 11:8–10).

The City by faith Abraham was waiting for – and which is awaited for by those who have put their faith and trust in Jesus – is the City of the living God, the Heavenly Jerusalem. In this City, it is expected that Abraham will join with…

> *…an innumerable company of angels, to the general assembly and church* [Community] *of the firstborn who are registered in heaven, to God the Judge of all, to the spirits of*

just men made perfect, to Jesus the Mediator of the new covenant, and to the blood of sprinkling that speaks better things than that of Abel. (Hebrews 12:22-24).

For Abraham, and all of God's people, for those who have trusted in God and in His Son the Lord Jesus and have replied **"YES"** to Wisdom's invitation, when they have completed the days which God has assigned to them, their rest is assured.

In the book of Hebrews – for which the writer is unknown but as Origen suggested in the third century: *"God alone knows"* – the writer explains what this rest consists of. The writer assures those who have come to believe in Jesus that a time will one day dawn when they will enter His rest. (Hebrew 4:3a). To continue with what the writer has stated, the significance of the Seventh Day is then addressed.

For He has spoken in a certain place of the seventh day in this way; "And God rested on the seventh day from all His works." (Hebrews 4:4). Quotation taken from Genesis 2:2.

The reader is then assured – and is also challenged.

There remains therefore a rest for the people of God. For he who has entered His rest has himself also ceased from his works as God did from His. Let us therefore be diligent to enter that rest. (Hebrews 4:9-11a).

With the emphasis in Hebrews chapter four on resting, the Seventh Day carries the same promised assurance as it does for those whose hope is in God. Meanwhile, in Matthew's gospel (11:25), we read of a prayer that Jesus prayed.

*"I thank you, Father, **Lord of heaven and earth**, that you have hidden these things from the wise and prudent and have revealed to babes."* i.e., The humble and the modest.

When Jesus spoke of His Father being *"Lord of heaven and earth"*, it was reminiscent of when Moses used exactly the same phrase when he addressed the children of Israel about choosing life and rest, rather than anxiety, turmoil and dust.

In Deuteronomy 28-30, Moses' words must rank as being the most important of his one hundred and twenty years. The final two verses form the culmination of his appeal.

> *"I call **heaven and earth** as witnesses today against you, that I have set before you life and death, blessing and cursing; therefore choose life, that both you and your descendants may live; that you may love the LORD your God, that you may obey His voice, and that you may cling to Him, for He is your life and the length of your days; and that you may dwell in the land which the LORD swore to your fathers, to Abraham, Isaac, and Jacob, to give them."* (Deuteronomy 30:19-20). Note especially Ecclesiastes 12:1-14.

For the children of Israel, after four hundred years of slavery in Egypt, the Promised Land was God's provision for it to become for them: *'Their Appointed Resting Place'*.

Before He prayed, Jesus rebuked those who were not willing to acknowledge and to confess their sin, but He then invited those who are prepared to do so, to follow Him.

> *"Come to Me, all you who labor and are heavy laden, and I will give you **rest**. Take My yoke upon you and learn from Me, for I am gentle and lowly in heart, and you will find **rest** for your souls. For my yoke is easy and My burden is light."* (Matthew 11:28-30).

Jesus knows what it means for those who follow Him, and especially if they place Him as their first choice as He guides them towards their desired haven. (See Psalm 107:23-32).

Being aware of what is involved when we devote our lives to Him, including suffering, Jesus encouraged His followers:

> "Let not your heart be troubled; you believe in God, believe also in Me. In My Father's house are many **mansions**; if it were not so, I would have told you. I go to prepare a place for you. And if I go and prepare a place for you, I will come again and receive you to Myself; that where I am, there you may be also." (John 14:1–3).

The temporary shelters that Jewish people make for their 'Sabbath-Rest' at the Feast of Tabernacles, when they give thanks for their end-of-year harvest, although they may be inferior (as the manger versus the Ark of the Covenant for some may have seemed inferior), corresponds to the many **'mansions'** Jesus referred to during His final hours with His disciples. When Jesus attended His last Feast of Tabernacles celebration in Jerusalem, He did so in order to announce:

> On the last day, that great day of the feast, Jesus stood and cried out, saying, "If anyone thirsts, let him come to Me and drink. He who believes in Me, as the Scripture has said, out of his heart will flow rivers of living water." (John 7:37–38).

The inference of what Jesus 'Cried Out' on the last day of the Feast of Tabernacles, recalled the Seventh Pillar of Wisdom.

> **"Forsake foolishness and live,
> and go in the way of understanding."** (Proverbs 9:6).

The Seventh Pillar of Wisdom is the harbinger of what Jesus 'Cried Out' out in the Temple in Jerusalem. But also, the Seventh Pillar, 'Love, Joy, Peace and Rest', is for the Gentiles from the nations (the Fifth Pillar) to be the recipients of faith in Jesus (albeit at times slowly due to a lack of understanding in accepting the advice of the Seventh Pillar of Wisdom).

For both Jews and Gentiles who have responded to Wisdom's invitation, it is because they have chosen *'Life'* and have been sanctified (made holy) by putting their faith in Jesus (as God likewise sanctified the Seventh Day by making it holy).

In his first letter to the Corinthians, Paul wrote to Gentiles who had little or no understanding of the Gospel. The extract which follows is how Paul described God's Plan of Salvation.

> *For you see your calling, brethren, that not many wise according to the flesh, not many mighty, not many noble, are called. But God has chosen the foolish things of the world to put to shame the wise, and God has chosen the weak things of the world to put to shame the things which are mighty; and the base things of the world and the things which are despised God has chosen, and the things which are not, to bring to nothing the things that are, that no flesh should glory in His presence. But of Him you are in Christ Jesus, who became for us **wisdom** from God – and righteousness and sanctification and redemption – that, as it is written, "He who glories, let him glory in the LORD."* (1 Corinthians 1:26–31).

THE SPIRIT OF WISDOM

The invitation of the Holy Spirit – The Spirit of Wisdom – is for those who trust in Jesus to attend the marriage supper of the Lamb of God (God's Passover Lamb), so that when He appears, His faithful ones will be able to join with Him.

Included as part of John's vision as it is described in the book of Revelation, there is a promise for those who have made themselves ready for the Bridegroom – the Lord Jesus.

> *Here is the patience of the saints; here are those who keep the commandments of God and the faith of Jesus. Then I*

*heard a voice from heaven saying to me, "Write: 'Blessed are the dead who die in the Lord from now on.'" "Yes," says the Spirit, "That they may **rest** from their labors, and their works follow them."* (Revelation 14:12–13).

When God ended His work then rested and *'Sanctified the Seventh Day'* in order to make it Holy– as Jewish people rest when their end-of-year harvest is completed at the time of the Feast of Tabernacles – God's reasoning appears (as promised for those who have put their faith and trust in Jesus), that they will also be able to experience what the Holy Spirit describes as: *"That they may **rest** from their labors."*

Eliyahu Lizorkin-Eyzebberg describes our resting in God as:

Not merely relaxation from exertion, but rather stationary rest – the absence of activity and movement.

In other words, to summarise what Jesus promised, that we might experience contentment for our bodies, minds and souls – less in the way of stress! – His promise confirms the salient design of the Seventh Pillar of Wisdom:

"Forsake foolishness and live,
and go in the way of understanding."

The parable Jesus selected when He addressed a group of Pharisees to explain the format of His Kingdom, was of a King's wedding festival. Taken from Matthew's Gospel, the following description is how Jesus explained His Kingdom.

"The kingdom of heaven is like a certain king who arranged a marriage for his son, and sent out his servants to call those who were invited to the wedding [those who received the first invitations]; *and they were not willing to come. Again, he sent out other servants, saying, 'Tell those who*

are invited, "See, I have prepared my dinner; my oxen and fatted cattle are killed, and all things are ready. Come to the wedding." ' "But they made light of it and went their ways, one to his own farm, another to his business. [See Luke 12:16-21]. *And the rest seized his servants, treated them spitefully, and killed them. But when the king heard about it, he was furious. And he sent out his armies, destroyed those murderers, and burned up their city."* [The Roman legions destroyed Jerusalem by fire in the year C.E. 70].

"Then he said to his servants, 'The wedding is ready, but those who were invited were not worthy. Therefore go into the highways, and as many as you find [Jews and Gentiles], *invite to the wedding.' So those servants went out into the highways and gathered together all whom they found, both bad and good. And the wedding hall was filled with guests. But when the king came in to see the guests, he saw a man there who did not have on a wedding garment. So he said to him, 'Friend, how did you come in here without a wedding garment?' And he was speechless. Then the king said to his servants, 'Bind him hand and foot, take him away, and cast him into outer darkness; there will be weeping and gnashing of teeth.' For many are called, but few are chosen."* (Matthew 22:2-14).

In His parable, Jesus stated what would happen to the Jewish people (the Fourth Pillar of Wisdom) – and later their city of Jerusalem should they cast Him aside. Invitations would then be sent to the Gentiles (the Fifth Pillar of Wisdom) so that if they respond, they would be welcomed as His guests. The absence of a wedding garment indicates a lack of holiness. *'Without holiness no one will see the Lord.'* (Hebrews 12:14). Holiness means: *'Sanctification'*. It is what God did when He *'Blessed the seventh day and sanctified it.'* (Genesis 2:3). i.e., God set the Seventh Day aside and made it Holy – knowing that His Creation would also need rest.

Jewish people have a long-held tradition that when their Messiah, the Christ, comes, there will be a great feast, such as a wedding feast. At the end when the wine is drunk, a toast will be given and they will cry out: *"l'chaim!"* (*"To Life!"*).

Sadly many Jewish people continue to believe that God has kept these things hidden from them. But this is not true, for they have only to take in what their ancient seer the prophet Isaiah said (in advance) about their Messiah, the Christ.

> *For unto us a Child is born, unto us a Son is given; and the government will be upon His shoulder. And His name will be called Wonderful, Counsellor, Mighty God, Everlasting Father, Prince of Peace. Of the increase of His government and peace there will be no end, upon the throne of David and over His kingdom, to order it and establish it with judgment and justice from that time forward, even forever. The zeal of the LORD of hosts will perform this.*
> (Isaiah 9:6-7).

"l'chaim!" is what the first Seven Days, the Seven Appointed Times of the LORD, and the Seven Pillars of Wisdom – my Master's Sevenfold Plan – was designed to achieve.

To bring to a close the Seventh Day, and for those who have chosen Jesus and rest, I felt it appropriate to do so with the closing words from Proverbs chapter eight. These lines – for they speak of the Lord Jesus as being the Master Craftsman – continue on from Proverbs 8:22-31 that I referred to during the First Day. (See page 58). They come immediately prior to the announcement of the Master's Seven Pillars of Wisdom as set-out down Proverbs 9:1-6.

For those who have made themselves ready by responding to *'Wisdom and Understanding'*, note the hint in this passage of the Bridegroom who is yet to come. It is here we are told that if there should be a delay in His coming, it is because the Father – as in the parable of the prodigal son (Luke 15:11–32) – is patient and forgiving, *'Waiting at the posts of His doors'* for His sons and His daughters to respond to His love. Is this not a reminder of the blood-stained doorposts in Egypt, and the cross on which Jesus died, that freedom from bondage and sin means we are set-free to worship God?

> *"Now, therefore, listen to me, my children,*
> *For blessed are those who keep my ways.*
> *Hear instruction and be wise,*
> *And do not disdain it.*
> *Blessed is the man who listens to me,*
> *Watching daily at my gates,*
> ***Waiting at the posts of my doors."***

> *"For whoever finds me finds life,*
> *And obtains favor from the* LORD*;*
> *But he who sins against me wrongs his own soul.*
> ***All those who hate me love death."***
> (Proverbs 8:32–36)

After suffering, the final seven words of Jesus must be heart-breaking as a result of those who say **"NO"** to His invitation. However it is a reminder of the consequences of ignoring Wisdom's advice. Therefore God says to those who seek Him and His *FREE* gift of eternal rest via His Son, the Lord Jesus:

> ***"Forsake foolishness and live,***
> ***and go in the way of understanding."***

To do so is to choose *'Life'* – the Lord Jesus – and the narrow path which leads to holiness and rest; rather than the broad path which results in dust and Sheol.

****

MY MASTER'S SEVENFOLD PLAN

God's Plan, that we are to be without blame before Him in love (Ephesians 1:4), is why Jesus said to Nicodemus, *"Most assuredly, I say to you, unless one is born again, he cannot see the kingdom of God."* (John 3:3). As with the Father, His Son and the Holy Spirit, God's Plan has three cardinal aspects. (1). The Seven Days of Creation. (2). The Seven Appointed Times of the LORD. (3). The Seven Pillars of Wisdom.

1. Jesus, at the time of a Passover observance – the First Appointed Time – Creation's *'Light'* was extinguished. After the Hebrew slaves had marked their homes with blood from their Passover lambs; they then became their evening meal. The evening before Jesus was also slain, He said to His disciples: *"The bread that I shall give is My flesh, which I shall give for the life of the world."* (John 6:51b). As God on the First Day said: *"Let there be light",* His Son, the *'Light'* and the *'Lamb of God'*, is the First Pillar of Wisdom.

2. Jesus, and Unleavened Bread, the Second Appointed Time – purification as manifested on the Second Day – yielded His life for others. The Second Pillar of Wisdom, Jesus' blood – *'for the life of all flesh is its blood'*– is evoked during the meal of Holy Communion. Red wine is symbolic of the life of Jesus which was in His blood.

3. Jesus, having died, three days later and at the time of His resurrection, appeared to His disciples at two tables supplied with food and drink. This, a Firstfruit Sign – the Third Appointed Time of the LORD – confirms that the resurrection of Jesus was in line with the Third Day and the Third Pillar of Wisdom: *'She has furnished her table.'*

4. Jesus, having told His disciples to remain in Jerusalem, sent the Holy Spirit at the time of the Feast of Weeks (Pentecost) – the Fourth Appointed Time of the LORD – to reap a spiritual harvest among Jewish people (Acts 2:41). The Fourth Pillar of Wisdom recalls when 3,000 Jewish people received the *'Dayspring from on High'* (the Fourth Day, the *'Dawn'*) into their lives and were baptised.

5. Jesus said: *"Salvation is of the Jews."* (John 4:22). His words recall the preaching of the Gospel by His disciples (Jews) to Gentiles, as in the sound of the Trumpet at the Feast of Trumpets, the Fifth Appointed Time of the LORD. Wisdom – the mentor of the Fifth Day – has upheld that the Gentiles are represented by the Fifth Pillar of Wisdom.

6. Jesus, *'The express image of His Father'* (Hebrews 1:3), invites us to dwell with Him in His Holy-of-Holies. On the Day of Atonement, the Sixth Appointed Time of the LORD, when Aaron entered the Holy-of-Holies to bow before the Ark of the Covenant, it represented God's dwelling place. When Mary placed Jesus in a manger, the manger depicted His dwelling place. The Sixth Day and the Sixth Pillar of Wisdom – **"Come, eat of my bread and drink of the wine I have mixed"** – confirms Jesus as the *'Son of God'* and *'Son of Man'* when He was born in Bethlehem. One thousand years earlier – i.e., *'**One Day**'* (2 Peter 3:8) – God said: *"You are My Son; today I became Your Father."* (Psalm 2:7).

7. Jesus, when He cried out *"It is finished!"* (John 19:30), His death recalled how when God *'finished'* His work, *'He rested on the Seventh Day.'* (Genesis 2:2). For those made blameless, when their lives come to an end, they will enter their rest. The Seventh Day, the Seventh Appointed Time, and the Seventh Pillar of Wisdom – **"Forsake foolishness and live, and go in the way of understanding"** – is that we might Tabernacle with Him in His holiness and glory.

THE MARRIAGE SUPPER OF GOD'S SON

Jesus' marriage supper – Jesus Son of God and Son of Man – is an end-time event which has been planned for from before the dawn of Creation. Its modus operandi is as follows.

1. The Father has gifted the food, seen in the *'Light'* of the First Day, for His Son's Bride. (The Bride is the redeemed of the nations: Jews and Gentiles).

2. The Father has gifted the drink, seen in the life-blood of His Son and poured out for His Son's Bride

3. The Father's table for His Son's wedding – today it is symbolised in the communion table – has been made ready from the Third Day of His Son's resurrection.

4. The Father's first guests, Jews who have been forgiven and cleansed – they have been made *'Holy'* – are dressed in garments of fine linen and have been made ready for the marriage supper of God's Son.

5. The Father's other guests, Gentiles who have been forgiven and cleansed – they have been made *'Holy'* – are dressed in garments of fine linen and have been made ready for the marriage supper of God's Son.

6. The Father's guests, those who are *'Born Again'*, are the offspring of God as well as the offspring of man.

7. The Father's Son speaks: *'Welcome, for you were dead and you are alive again; you were lost and you are found. Come, enter into My rest.'* (See Luke 15:20-32).

When John the evangelist who had born witness to the Word of God and the testimony of Jesus was in exile on the island of Patmos, he heard a loud voice which came directly from the throne-room of God, saying to him:

"Praise our God, all you His servants and those who fear Him, both small and great!"

And I heard, as it were, the voice of a great multitude, as the sound of many waters and as the sound of mighty thunderings, saying,

"Alleluia! For the Lord God Omnipotent reigns! Let us be glad and rejoice and give Him glory, for the marriage of the Lamb has come, and His wife has made herself ready."

And to her it was granted to be arrayed in fine linen, clean and bright, for the fine linen is the righteous acts of the saints.

Then He said to me,

"Write; 'Blessed are those who are called to the marriage supper of the Lamb!' "

And he said to me,

"These are the true sayings of God."

(Revelation 19:5-9).

****

A. WISEMAN

Two weeks after I first became aware that the Seven Days of Creation, followed later by the Seven Appointed Times of the LORD, that they resemble a similar theme, I was introduced in a hotel in Tel Aviv, Israel, to Dr. Allen Wiseman, a Canadian-born Jew who has a doctorate in Jewish philosophy.

Dr. Wiseman told me he had just recently completed a paper about the links connecting the Seven Days of Creation with the Seven Appointed Times of the LORD. The following four paragraphs are taken from Dr. A. Wiseman's essay.

God's Seven Holy Appointed Times [The Hebrew peoples' Seven Annual Biblical Feasts], mark the yearly Biblical calendar. God initiated the series in Exodus chapter twelve, to be fully listed in Leviticus chapter twenty three.

These Times represent a pattern of Scripture that begins with the seven days or periods of Creation week, which are echoed by the regular weekly cycle, and further elaborated in Israel's deliverance from Egyptian slavery. As Creation continues until the end of time, so do the effects of these seven feasts.

Both the repetition of the weekly cycle and these seven yearly holidays, remind us of real past events, which also point to the prophetic future. As such, these feasts are more than ordinary holidays. While the regular weekly and yearly cycles ingrain in us a down-to-earth rhythm in life, the linear process gives us an overall perspective that spans from the very beginning of Creation to the ultimate completion of GOD's redemptive purposes.

Historically, because the Christian world veered away from its Jewish roots in the early centuries, the larger scope and significance of the LORD's seven feasts were often overlooked, or not sufficiently understood.

Never before (or since) have I been introduced to a Jewish man who, when he was born, was named: A. Wiseman. And that this should have taken place in Israel just fourteen days after I had come to see how the Seven Days of Creation and the Seven Appointed Times of the LORD, that they have such vivid resemblance to each other, was simply awesome.

Of course I thanked God for my meeting with Dr. A. Wiseman, for it enabled me to understand these seven connections – plus the Seven Pillars of Wisdom (their vital importance as illustrated by my aircraft's wiring diagrams) – which together forms the blueprint of my Master's Sevenfold Plan.

****

THE SARAJEVO HAGGADAH

In seeking to explain my Master's Sevenfold Plan, I thought it appropriate if I were to include a mention of the Sarajevo Haggadah; an illuminated Jewish manuscript that is believed to be the oldest surviving Sephardic Haggadah in the world. This particular Haggadah is thought to have been assembled in Spain in the first half of the fourteenth century.

A Haggadah is a Jewish prayer book that is used during the festival of Passover. Written and illustrated in Hebrew, the Sarajevo Haggadah outlines the Passover rituals in which special foods are eaten; songs are sung; stories are told; and the concept of freedom is celebrated.

This Haggadah (The word Haggadah means: *'A Narrative'*) is thought to have originated in a Hebrew text which was assembled to tell Jewish children the story of their redemption.

> *And you shall tell your son in that day, saying, "This is done because of what the LORD did for me when I came up from Egypt."* (Exodus 13:8).

According to Jeremy Norman's on-line web-site, HISTORY OF INFORMATION, this particular Haggadah is considered to be the most beautiful illuminated Haggadah in existence.

The Sarajevo Haggadah was produced in the mid-14th century in Barcelona, Spain. It was written on bleached calfskin and illuminated in copper and gold and opens with thirty four pages of illustrations of scenes from Creation through to the death of Moses.

Its pages are stained with wine – evidence that it has been used at many Passover Seders – and it is now preserved at the National Museum of Bosnia and Herzegovina in Sarajevo.

The Sarajevo Haggadah has survived many close calls with destruction. Historians believe that it was taken out of Spain by Spanish Jews who were expelled by the Alhambra Decree of 1492. Notes in the margins of the Haggadah indicate that it surfaced in Italy in the 16th century. It was sold in 1894 to the National Museum in Sarajevo by a man whose name was Joseph Kohen.

During World War Two, the manuscript was kept hidden from the Nazis by the Museum's chief librarian, Dervis Korkut, who at risk to his own life smuggled the Haggadah out of Sarajevo. Korkut then gave it to a Muslim cleric in Zenica, where it was believed to have been hidden under the floorboards of a mosque, or a Muslim home.

During the Bosnian War of the early 1990s, when Sarajevo was under constant siege by Bosnian Serb forces, the manuscript survived in an underground bank vault. In order to quell rumours that the government had sold the Haggadah to buy weapons, in 1995, the president of Bosnia presented the manuscript at a Jewish community Seder.

In 2001, the manuscript was restored through a special campaign financed by the United Nations and the Bosnian Jewish community. It then went on permanent display at a museum in December 2002.

Its monetary value is undetermined, but a museum in Spain required that it be insured for $7 million before it could be transported to an exhibition in Spain. What is fascinating about this ancient Jewish relic is that the artisan who assembled the Sarajevo Haggadah has portrayed in the first eight illustrations, the events of the first seven days as they are described in the Bible.

In his book, FESTIVAL STUDIES – BEING THOUGHTS ON THE JEWISH YEAR (First published in 1906), its author, Israel Abrahams M.A., describes the artisan's depiction of the first account of Creation.

The first day [the first picture] depicts chaos; the Spirit of God hovers as a golden flame, rising from primeval waters. Next [still the First Day] comes the separation between light and darkness. Under a round arch, the space is divided into two halves by a vertical line, to the left of which a deep black patch indicates the darkness, while to the right a far paler patch represents the light.

In the third picture [now the Second Day], the separation between the waters is portrayed; from the sky there stream downwards bright rays, emblematic, doubtless, of the Divine influence.

The fourth picture [concluding the first folio of the first four illustrations and representing the work of the Third Day] repeats, as do the sixth and seventh pictures, these streaming rays which descend from above in the shape of a spreading cone. In this fourth picture, we are shown the separation of water from land, the earth bristling with trees and shrubs. [i.e., The emergence/resurrection of plant life].

Fifthly, there is the work of the fourth day; the Sun and Moon and Stars appear above the picture proper, and are repeated in the sixth picture.

Birds are at the top of the round globe, fish at the bottom [the Fifth day], while between are the wild beasts amid which a lion occupies a prominent place.

The seventh picture [the Sixth Day] repeats several of the previous details, but adds the creation of man, a somewhat dwarfed figure.

Finally in the eighth picture, appears a unique illustration. In the picture to which I refer, we see a human figure, young and beard-less, clothed in an ample robe, hooded and red. The figure is seated in repose under a *'Trefoil Canopy'* – and this figure is apparently meant to represent God. The editors of the Sarajevo Haggadah feel no doubt whatever that such is the artist's intention.

If so, the picture is unique, or at all events a great rarity, and proves conclusively one of two things.

(1) The artist was a Christian, or more probably,

(2) The artist was a Jew, copying slavishly a Christian model, the un-Jewish character of which was, for some reason, not perceived by him.

In heraldry, a *'Trefoil Canopy'* is usually made up of three rounded and slightly pointed leaves, set in a formal way at the three upper extremities of a small cross, the lower end which ends in various ways like roots buried in the ground.

It would seem from Israel Abrahams' conclusion about this rare and valuable item, that if God is indeed being portrayed in art form as a man – *'So God created man in His own image; in the image of God, He created him...'* (Genesis 1:27); and Jesus, who, according to St. Paul, *'He is the image of the invisible God, the firstborn over all creation'* (Colossians 1:15), – then it is not erroneous to see that not only God and the Holy Spirit, but also Jesus is being portrayed in the Bible's first account of Creation. And is not the *'Trefoil Canopy'* and its *'Cross'*, pointing us in a similar way to Jesus and His cross?

If this is what the artisan had intended to portray, that God and *not* man is the subject of the first seven days (as I have suggested in this study), then the first account of Creation may have more to do with God's Son and His Bride (the Church), than it has to do with Adam and his bride (Eve).

Regarding Creation, the Rev. Adolph Saphir has said:

The great object [purpose] of Creation is to glorify God in the redemption and sanctification of His people.

It is also important to recall the Haggadah's odyssey. The likelihood of a fourteenth century Jewish sage designing and making the Sarajevo Haggadah (about one hundred years before the Spanish inquisition of 1482), then later other Jews taking it out of Spain for safe keeping because of persecution, would this not have been a wise decision, and why the Sarajevo Haggadah has been preserved for posterity for more than six hundred and seventy years?

The reason why Jewish people would have been anxious to preserve this ancient document is because they knew of its importance when they observed the Passover. For Jewish people, their Seven Holy Appointed Times of the LORD are integral to the way they understand and observe Scripture. Therefore, for God, His Son and the Holy Spirit, to be portrayed as the focus of the first Seven Days, is well within the portals of Jewish and Gentile doctrine and belief in God.

THE SPANISH INQUISITION

The reason for the Spanish inquisition against Jewish people was to ensure that for those who had converted from Judaism to Catholicism, that they had done so correctly. This regulation was intensified after two royal decrees (1492 and 1501) were issued ordering the Jews to choose baptism or exile.

The Spanish inquisition must have been truly terrifying. At first those involved were encouraged to attend a tribunal voluntarily so they could confess their heresies for which they would receive a lighter punishment. However, this did not mean an end to their troubles. Many were forced to become informants of their families, friends and neighbours. Once an individual had been accused and the presence of so-called heresy established, they may then have been imprisoned and their property confiscated in order to cover expenses and maintenance costs. The time they spent in prison would have lasted for months; or in some cases for many years.

Various methods of torture were used to extract confessions; as opposed to a punishment in its own right. It is known that little distinction was given to those who were tortured, with women, children, the infirm and the aged not being exempted from punishment.

Punishments ranged from wearing a penitential garment (and for many a yellow star as happened during the Second World War) for various lengths of time – in some cases for the rest of their lives – to acts of penance, lashings; or in the case of unrepentant or relapsed heretics, burning at the stake.

In the wake of the first decree, more than 160,000 Jews were forced to leave Spain. Anybody suspected of being a heretic was investigated, and this applied even to those who had converted to Catholicism. Of those who were forced to leave Spain because of persecution, Dr. J. H. Hertz of the office of the Chief Rabbi – circa 1917 – recalls one personal account which was recorded on the 3rd of August, 1492.

> *The Spanish noon is a blaze of azure fire, and the dusty pilgrims crawl like an endless serpent along treeless plains and bleached high roads, through rock-split ravines and castellated, cathedral-shadowed towns.*

The hoary patriarch, wrinkled as an almond shell, bows painfully upon his staff. The beautiful young mother, ivory-pale, well-nigh swoons beneath her burden; in her large enfolding arms nestles her sleeping babe, round her knees flock her little ones with bruised and bleeding feet. "Mother, shall we soon be there?"

The halt, the blind, are amid the train. Sturdy pack-horses laboriously drag the tented wagons wherein lie the sick athirst with fever. The panting mules are urged forward by spur and goad; stuffed are the heavy saddle-bags with the wreckage of ruined homes. Hark to the tinkling silver bells that adorn the tenderly carried silken scrolls.

Noble and abject, learned and simple, illustrious and obscure, plod side by side, all brothers now, all merged in one routed army of misfortune. Woe to the straggler who falls by the way-side! No friend shall close his eyes.

They leave behind the grape, the olive, and the fig; the vines they planted, the corn they sowed, the garden-cities of Andalusia and Aragon, Estremadura and La Mancha, of Granada and Castile; the altar, the hearth, and the grave of their fathers. The townsman spits at their garments, the shepherd quits his flock, the peasant his plough, to pelt with curses and stones, the villager sets on their trail his yelping cur. Oh, the weary march! Oh, the up-torn roots of home! Oh the blankness of the receding goal!

Listen to their lamentations:

"They that ate dainty food are desolate in the streets; they that were reared in scarlet embrace dunghills. They flee away and wander about. Men say among the nations, 'They shall no more sojourn there; our end is near, our days full, our doom is come.'" (Lamentations 4:5, 15 & 18).

Under such harsh and painful conditions, it is understandable why this rare and valued Haggadah was taken out of Spain.

Thankfully it has survived, and since its restoration it has been used as a valuable teaching aid to assist in the telling of the Biblical account of Creation and the Passover observance, the time when Jesus gave Himself unreservedly for others – even those alive today.

****

THOU DIDST LEAVE THY THRONE

For my epilogue, I have chosen a hymn by Elizabeth Emily Steele Elliott that was published in 1864. This hymn features many of the life aspects of Jesus I have included in this study.

Thou didst leave Thy throne
And Thy kingly crown,
When Thou camest to earth for me;
But in Bethlehem's home
Was there found no room
For Thy holy nativity:
O come to my heart, Lord Jesus;
There is room in my heart for Thee.

Heaven's arches rang
When the angels sang,
Proclaiming Thy royal degree:
But of lowly birth
Cam'st Thou, Lord, on earth,
And in great humility:
O come to my heart, Lord Jesus;
There is room in my heart for Thee.

The foxes found rest,
And the birds their nest,
In the shade of the cedar-tree;
But Thy couch was the sod,
O Thou Son of God,
In the deserts of Galilee:
O come to my heart, Lord Jesus;
There is room in my heart for Thee.

Thou camest, O Lord,
With the living word
That should set Thy people free;
But, with mocking scorn,
And with crown of thorn,
They bore Thee to Calvary:
O come to my heart, Lord Jesus;
There is room in my heart for Thee.

When heaven's arches ring,
And her choirs sing,
At Thy coming to victory,
Let Thy voice call me home,
Saying, Yet there is room,
There is room at My side for thee!
And my heart shall rejoice, Lord Jesus,
When Thou comest and callest for me.

****

BIBLIOGRAPHY

Abrahams, Israel M.A. FESTIVAL STUDIES. Reader in Talmudic to the University of Cambridge. Macmillan and Co Limited, London. Published in 1906

Allen-Piper, John. CREATION UNLIMITED. Grosvenor House Publishing Ltd. Published in 2020.

Barker, Margaret. CHRISTMAS THE ORIGINAL STORY. Published by: The Society for Promoting Christian Knowledge (SPCK 2008). 36, Causton Street, London, SW1P 4ST.

Bartholomew, Craig G. and O'Dowd, Ryan P. OLD TESTAMENT WISDOM LITERATURE. Published in 2011 by: The Inter Varsity Press, P.O. Box 1400, Downers Grove, IL 60515-1426, USA.

Bullinger, E.W. D. D. FIGURES OF SPEECH USED IN THE BIBLE. (1898). Published by: Messers Eyre & Spottiswoode, Great New Street, London. And: Messers E & J. B. Young & Co., Cooper Union, Fourth Avenue, New York.

Bullinger, E. W. D. D. NUMBER IN SCRIPTURE. Reprint. Published in 1967 by: Kregel Publications, a division of Kregel, Inc., P.O. Box 2607, Grand Rapids, MI 49501.

Bridges, Charles (1794–1869), PROVERBS – THE GENEVA SERIES OF COMMENTARIES. Published in 1846.

Cox, Professor Brian. BBC Television Series: WONDERS OF THE SOLAR SYSTEM – ORDER OUT OF CHAOS.

Dalman D.D., Professor Gustaf. JESUS-JESHUA, STUDIES IN THE GOSPELS. The Authorised Translation carried out by the Rev. Paul P. Levertoff. Society for Promoting Christian Knowledge (S.P.C.K.). First published in the English language in 1929. Published in New York and Toronto.

Davis, David. THE ELIJAH LEGACY – The Life and Times of Elijah. The Prophetic Significance for Israel, Islam and the Church in the Last Days. Published in 2012.

Henry, Matthew. MATTHEW HENRY'S COMMENTARY ON THE WHOLE BIBLE. 1706. Marshall Morgan & Scott, Ltd. 1–5 Portpool Lane, Holborn, E.C.1. Edited by Rev. Leslie F. Church, Ph.D, F.R. Hist.S. My edition published in 1960.

Hertz Dr. J. H. Chief Rabbi. Circa 1917. A BOOK OF JEWISH THOUGHTS. Revised Edition. Office of the Chief Rabbi. London. My edition published in June 1943.

Kenyon, Dr. E. W. THE BLOOD COVENANT. Kenyon's Gospel Publishing Society. Published in 1969.

Lane, Eric. PSALMS VOLUMES 1 & 2. Focus on the Bible Commentary Series. Published in 2006.

Lizorkin-Eyzebberg, Eliyahu. BECOMING ISRAEL.

Norman, Jeremy. Norman's web-site, HISTORY OF INFORMATION.

Pink, A. W. P. GLEANINGS IN GENESIS. (Watchmaker 1951). Digitalized by Watchmaker Publishing. All Rights Reserved.

Sacks, Dr. Stuart D. REVEALING JESUS AS MESSIAH. Published in 1998 by Christian Focus Publications Ltd. Geanies House, Fearn, Ross-shire, IV20 1TW, Scotland.

Saphir, Rev. Adolph B.A. (1831–1891). CHRIST AND THE SCRIPTURES. Morgan and Chase, 38 Ludgate Hill, London.

Stibbs, Alan (1901–1971). HIS BLOOD WORKS. Christian Focus Publications, Geanies House, Fearn, Ross-shire, Scotland, IV20 1TW. First published in 1962.

Wiseman, A. Dr. THE FEASTS – SEVEN HOLY APPOINTED TIMES OF THE LORD.

Wright, Nicholas Thomas. JOHN FOR EVERYONE. Society for Promoting Christian Knowledge (SPCK). 36, Causton Street, London, SW1P 4ST. First published in 2002.

Young, Dr. Brad H. JESUS THE JEWISH THEOLOGIAN. Henderson Publisher inc. Peabody, Massachusetts. First Published in 1995.

****